PRINCETON STUDIES IN INTERNATIONAL FINANCE

No. 75, November 1993

THE GERMAN BUYBACKS, 1932-1939:
A CURE FOR OVERHANG?

ADAM KLUG

INTERNATIONAL FINANCE SECTION

DEPARTMENT OF ECONOMICS
PRINCETON UNIVERSITY
PRINCETON, NEW JERSEY

INTERNATIONAL FINANCE SECTION
EDITORIAL STAFF

Peter B. Kenen, *Director*

Margaret B. Riccardi, *Editor*

Lillian Spais, *Editorial Aide*

Lalitha H. Chandra, *Subscriptions and Orders*

Library of Congress Cataloging-in-Publication Data

Klug, Adam.
The German buybacks, 1932-1939 : a cure for overhang? / Adam Klug.
p. cm. — (Princeton studies in international finance, ISSN 0081-8070 ; no. 75)
Includes bibliographical references.
ISBN 0-88165-247-4 (pbk.) : $11.00
1. Debt relief—Germany—History—20th century. 2. Debt equity
conversion—Germany—History—20th century. I. Title. II. Series.
HJ8654.K58 1993
336.3'6'094309043—dc20   93-21277
                                                                              CIP

Printed in the United States of America by Princeton University Printing Services at Princeton, New Jersey

International Standard Serial Number: 0081-8070
International Standard Book Number: 0-88165-247-4
Library of Congress Catalog Card Number: 93-21277

CONTENTS

TABLES

FIGURES

1 INTRODUCTION

In December 1936, the U.S. commercial attaché in Berlin reported that the Nazi government was making changes in the capital structure of the giant Ruhr utility, the Rheinische-Westphalisches Elektrizitäts Gesellschaft. He pointed out, however, that there was no special reason for American concern, for, of a $10 million loan that had once been floated by the firm in the United States, all but $2.5 million had been repurchased. The mortgage bond that had guaranteed the issue under the law of the state of New York had not prevented these buybacks. Indeed, as the Germans had long pointed out, there was nothing illegal about them[1]—an aspect that distinguished them from repurchases of debt in the 1980s, which required explicit creditor permission. Many such buybacks took place in the 1930s. They differed from the negotiated or donor-financed repurchases of the 1980s in that they were carried out in large measure by private firms, albeit with official permission under an exchange-control regime. In addition, many buybacks were not performed for cancellation but were undertaken by parties other than the original issuers in order to re-register the bonds for trading on the Berlin stock exchange.[2]

The Existing Literature

Although the importance of the German buyback program was discussed

This research has been generously supported by the Deutscher Akademischer Austauschdienst and the International Finance Section of the Department of Economics, Princeton University. I thank Udo Broll and Professor Hans-Jürgen Vosgerau for their hospitality during a stay at the University of Konstanz. I also thank, for their assistance, the archivists Frau Maiberg, of the Bundesarchiv Koblenz, Ben Primer and Jean Holliday, of the Seeley G. Mudd Library, Princeton, Elizabeth Ogburn, of the Bank of England, Rosemary Lazenby, of the Federal Reserve Board of New York, and Bill Creech, of the National Archives, Washington.

I have benefited greatly from discussions with the following people and from their comments on earlier drafts: Stijn Claessens, Ishac Diwan, Bill English, M. June Flanders, Harold James, David Laidler, Choon-Geol Moon, Albrecht Ritschl, Kenneth Rogoff, and seminar participants at the University of Illinois at Urbana-Champaign, Indiana University-Purdue University at Indianapolis, Princeton University, Rutgers University, the University of Western Ontario, and the Research Department of the International Monetary Fund. All errors are, of course, mine.

[1] NA RG151 C 600, Germany, "Commercial Attaché Miller to Domeratsky," December 14, 1936; AA SW, Finanzielle Beziehungen mit der USA, "Ritter Telegram," January 26, 1934.

[2] A decision of the German Economics Ministry in late 1933 to permit trading on the

1

in some accounts at the time (Ellis, 1941, pp. 186-187, 195), most contemporary academic discussions of the Nazi government's external economic policies concentrated on its dangerously novel system of exchange control and its autarkic import restrictions (Bonnell, 1940; Ellis, 1941).[3] Several recent studies of the 1930s debt crisis show that past episodes of buybacks provide insight into contemporary policy problems (Eichengreen and Lindert, 1989; Eichengreen, 1991), but research by Garber (1990) and English (1991) suggests that the first studies of this type have not exhausted the questions that might be asked. The studies have not, moreover, dealt with Germany, which was the major defaulter in the 1930s, or attempted to resolve the debate sparked by Bulow and Rogoff (1988) regarding the desirability of buybacks. The 1930s South American defaults studied by Jorgensen and Sachs (1989) are not, in fact, the most appropriate examples to use when assessing the desirability of buybacks from a debtor country's standpoint; the market for the South American bonds was extremely thin, and Jorgensen and Sachs were able to study only 28 bond issues bought back by four countries over a period of 15 to 20 years. (I present below statistical evidence on 96 German issues repurchased in only 2 years.) None of the earlier studies, moreover, presents archival evidence regarding the debtor's motivation for buying back debt. In addition, the discussion of the creditors' views has been limited to those of Britain (Eichengreen and Portes, 1989a, 1989c), even though the United States was the major creditor.

Germany as a Test Case for Recent Theory

Table 1 demonstrates the importance of the German case. In 1930, Germany was, after Canada, the largest single long-term borrower from the United States, and it was by far the largest defaulter on U.S. loans. Germany alone accounted for 8.7 percent of total U.S. long-term portfolio investment. By comparison, all of South America, which has figured almost exclusively in previous studies, accounted for 19.4 percent. Table 2, taken from the confidential figures used by the State Department, shows that German long-term indebtedness to all other

---

Berlin bourse of 43 bond issues formerly floated on Wall Street was known to the U.S. State Department: NA RG59 862.51/3839, "Memorandum on Converted Dollar Bonds" (referring to conversions performed in January 1934), n.d.

[3] Schuker (1988, pp. 70-75) and James (1986, chap. 10) contain recent accounts of the early phases of the buyback process but are not concerned with the economic consequences of the buybacks.

countries was just slightly higher than its indebtedness to the United States, and the distribution of its short-term indebtedness was almost equal to its long-term debt. These facts, coupled with the large size of the German buybacks, give special interest to the German case, which can demonstrate what might happen today if a major debtor in partial default, such as Brazil, were to try to repurchase a significant proportion of its debt. It may also help us to evaluate models that give conflicting predictions about scenarios of that sort.

In the ensuing discussion, I shall be concerned in particular with the argument of Bulow and Rogoff (1988, 1991) that, when the marginal value of a country's debt is below the average market price, the only effect of a buyback at the market price will be a financial transfer from the debtor to the creditor, because the buyback will raise the market price. This conclusion reflects the assumption by Bulow and Rogoff that the marginal value of the debt indicates its true value to the debtor country. Buybacks can be justified within the Bulow-Rogoff framework, but only if the creditor and debtor attach different valuations to the defaulted debt (Claessens and Diwan, 1989).[4] Arguments based on differences in the valuation of partly defaulted debt will be of particular interest in the discussion that follows, because German documents contemporary to the operations, especially those that were secret or confidential, can be used to reveal the subjective valuations placed on German debt. These records also provide an indirect way to test the usefulness of the game-theory framework adopted in some theoretical analyses of buybacks; we shall see whether they can be used to demonstrate that a particular strategy was played in response to a real or imagined threat by another player.

Outline of the Findings

The present study provides evidence that, as with the Bolivian debt in

---

[4] The well-known model of Krugman (1989) depends on the disincentive effects on investment of a large debt overhang. These effects can justify a buyback if good or bad states can occur after the buyback. The debtor is better off in the good state, because the debtor keeps the incremental income from the debt reduction resulting from a buyback. The creditor is better off in the bad state, because the buyback makes it more likely that the debtor will be able to meet its remaining obligations. Hence, both parties can gain in terms of expected utility. I do not assess this argument because the two-state framework cannot be clearly related to the historical case under study. The Kenen (1991) version of the debt-overhang scenario will figure below because it is based on the possibility of trade retaliation, which affects the debtor and creditor asymmetrically. In Kenen's model, a buyback can be beneficial to both debtor and creditor because it postpones the date of debt repudiation; the mutuality of gain does not depend on a difference between the marginal valuations of the debt by the debtor and creditor.

3

1988, the market value of Germany's debt rose during the period of buyback activity. It also demonstrates, however, that this outcome does not decisively confirm the Bulow-Rogoff conclusion, because regression analysis does not connect it to the buyback. Accordingly, I conclude that the large buybacks of German debt did not cause a significant increase in the market value of the remaining debt and thus did not benefit the creditor at the debtor's expense. This conclusion is reinforced by evidence that German policymakers, knowing that Germany was not going to repudiate its debt, as its creditors feared, and having reasons of their own for not cutting all links with the international capital market, consistently valued the debt above its market price. The difference of opinion about the likelihood of repudiation was genuine. Nevertheless, I shall argue that Germany could not have gained merely because of the subjective difference in valuation. That would have been possible only if Germany could have kept the buybacks secret. In fact, I find that the creditors had managed to acquire enough information to forecast future bond prices.

I also find that the buybacks can be explained by the particular actions threatened by the creditors in the event of default. Those of the United States had more effect than those of other creditor countries, because the United States threatened Germany with a trade embargo in the event of default, whereas other creditor countries threatened only to expropriate German trade revenues. Expropriation affects the debtor and creditor symmetrically—that is, the former's loss is the latter's gain—hence, it cannot produce a difference in subjective valuation. Trade disruption, by contrast, was regarded at the time as being harmful to Germany but not beneficial to the United States. It was thus bound to produce a difference in subjective valuation and more scope for mutually beneficial buybacks.

Chapter 2 of this study describes German methods of debt reduction. It provides new information on the nature, timing, and extent of the buybacks, demonstrating that the operation was by far the largest of its kind in history. Chapter 3 analyzes the effect of the buybacks on the secondary-market price of the debt. Chapter 4 discusses German motives, emphasizing that German policy was driven primarily by a valuation of the debt different from that of Germany's creditors, deriving in particular from Germany's secret decision not to repudiate and from the American threat of trade disruption. Chapter 5 concludes the study.

2 GERMAN DEBT HISTORY IN THE 1930s

This chapter describes the size and composition of the German debt and the methods of debt reduction used by Germany. It shows that previous accounts have understated the importance and duration of the debt repurchases.

The Size and Nature of the Debt

Table 1 shows the importance of long-term loans to Germany in the total U.S. portfolio. It should be read by comparing investment in Germany with investment in the global regions and in Canada. Total portfolio investment is shown to be almost as high in Germany as in the whole of South America, and higher than in the whole of Asia. Although South America was the major area in default on U.S. loans in the 1930s, the loans were not concentrated in any one country. Thus, Germany was the single largest defaulting country. Table 2, taken from the confidential figures used by the State Department, can be used in conjunction with the figure for the total stock of world debt, approximately $34,000 million,[5] to show that the German share of total world

TABLE 1

U.S. LONG-TERM FOREIGN INVESTMENT, DECEMBER 1930
(*in millions of dollars*)

	Direct Investment	Portfolio Investment	Total Investment	Percent of World Total
Germany	244	1,117	1,361	8.7
Europe	1,468	3,461	4,929	31.4
Canada	2,049	1,893	3,942	25.1
South America	1,631	1,411	3,042	19.4
Asia	420	1,023	1,443	9.2
All other	2,273	46	2,319	14.8
Total world	7,841	7,834	15,675	100.0

SOURCE: Royal Institute of International Affairs, 1937.

---

[5] I have found no figure for total world debt in 1932. For 1931, however, it was estimated by the Royal Institute of International Affairs (1937, p. 222) to be £7,000 million ($34,020 million).

TABLE 2

GEOGRAPHICAL DISTRIBUTION OF GERMAN DEBT, MAY 1932
(in millions of reichsmarks and dollars)

Country	Short-Term Credits	%	Long-Term Credits	%	Total Credits	%
United States	3,227 ($770)	31.8	5,165 ($1,230)	49.3	8,392 ($2,000)	40.7
Netherlands	1,661	16.4	1,914	18.3	3,575	17.3
Switzerland	1,615	15.9	1,146	10.9	2,761	13.4
Great Britain	1,286	12.7	1,129	10.8	2,415	11.7
France	474	4.7	482	4.6	956	4.6
Sweden	136	1.3	167	1.6	303	1.5
Belgium	119	1.2	80	0.8	199	1.0
Czechoslovakia	157	1.5	18	0.2	175	0.8
Italy	73	0.7	74	0.7	147	0.7
Denmark	51	0.5	9	0.1	60	0.3
Norway	14	0.1	5	0.0	19	0.1
Others	1,340	13.2	281	2.7	1,621	7.9
Total	10,153 ($2,418)	100.0	10,470 ($2,494)	100.0	20,623 ($4,912)	100.0

SOURCE: NA RG59 862.51/3636, "Memorandum from the Office of the Economic Advisor," May 1, 1933.
NOTE: Dollar equivalents are given as they appear in the document.

TABLE 3

GERMAN LONG-TERM FOREIGN INDEBTEDNESS BY TYPE OF CREDIT GRANTED, FEBRUARY 1932
(in millions of reichsmarks)

Type of Obligation	Reich, States, & Other Public Bodies	Reichsbank & Golddiskont-bank	Credit Banks	Industry, Commerce, Communications, Agriculture, etc.	Other German Debtors	Total
Foreign-currency bonds issued abroad	3,484	—	1,114	3,202	124	7,924
Mortgages	12	—	29	345	147	533
Long-term advances	29	—	199	1,229	123	1,580
Other long-term debt	—	—	164	164	115	433
Total	3,525	—	4,940	4,940	509	10,470

SOURCE: NA RG59 862.51/3636, "Memorandum from the Office of the Economic Advisor," May 1, 1933.

TABLE 4

DISTRIBUTION BY SECTOR OF GERMAN BONDS
ISSUED IN THE UNITED STATES, JUNE 1932
(*in millions of dollars*)

Sector	Value
Official bodies	
(Reich, states, and provinces)	358
Municipalities	168
Agricultural and state banks	185
Utilities	265
Electrical engineering	87
Metals	146
Shipping	32
Banks	45
Others	42
Total	1,327

SOURCE: Calculated from the *Frankfurter Zeitung und Handelsblatt, Börsen und Wirtschafts
Kalender 1933.*

debt was about 14 percent in 1932. Table 2 also shows that the American share of long-term loans to Germany was preponderant at 49.3 percent, with the Netherlands having the next highest share at 18.3 percent. This reflects the large scale of U.S. commercial lending in the 1920s (see Schuker, 1988, and McNeil, 1986, for the history, and Klug, 1990, for an economic analysis).

As to the types of debt outstanding, Table 3 shows that 31 percent of the total long-term debt represented bond issues by industry, commerce, and agriculture, and 33 percent represented bond issues by public bodies. Table 4, calculated from the *Frankfurter Zeitung's* financial supplement for 1933, presents a further breakdown of indebtedness by type of borrower. It shows that 13 percent of German bond issues outstanding were, in fact, municipal debts, a category subsumed under "Public Bodies" in the previous table. Private industrial issues accounted for only 17 percent of the total, the issues of public utilities being about as large. The industrial issues were also concentrated in heavy industry, with iron and steel accounting for $135 million of this group. Agricultural loans were also significant, but they were largely owed by the quasi-public Rentenbank-Creditanstalt, the debt of which alone was $102 million.

8

Pressures on the Debtors

Although the Hoover moratorium of July 1931 had suspended reparations payments, the German government promised to maintain interest
and amortization payments on foreign bonds denominated in foreign
currencies.[6] The short-term loans were covered by the standstill agreement, which gave Germany continued access to trade credit in exchange for reduced, but still considerable, servicing of the short-term
bank loans.[7]

Yet matters with regard to the long-term debt were not entirely
under the government's control. Spokesmen for debtor companies and
institutions pointed out that the agreements made between the German
government and its creditors at the July 1931 London Conference
effectively allowed private-sector debtors to default on their debts
without giving their creditors legal recourse in the German courts.[8]
The financial position of German industry gradually improved during
1932, but the foreign debts were heavily concentrated on companies
and institutions that were still threatened by bankruptcy. The iron and
steel industry, badly hurt by the collapse of its exports, could not pay
its debts without government subsidies (Berkenkopf, 1932). Profits for
the manufacturing industry did not recover for 1932 as a whole, and
those for the utilities (water, gas, and electricity) remained below the
1930 level and well below that for 1929 (James, 1986, table 30, p. 284).
The shipping companies, with $31.5 million owed in the United States,
were also in danger of default because the devaluation of sterling in
1931 had given an advantage to their British competition (Krogmann,
1977, p. 60). The agricultural banks, major debtors as we have seen,
remained insolvent until bailed out by the new regime in 1933.[9] Thus,
irrespective of the decisions of the Reich government, many individual
debtors threatened default, and they formed a committee to negotiate
a cut in their debt-service payments.[10] In 1933, however, new political
factors shifted the locus of the financial crisis. The Hitler cabinet

[6] "Finance Minister Dietrich Assures World Germany Will Meet Private Debts," *The
New York Times*, January 1, 1932.
[7] See James (1985) and Forbes (1987) for detailed discussions of the standstill, and
Childs (1958, pp. 20-23) on the long-term debt.
[8] "Liquidation der Auslandsschulden," *Wirtschaftsdienst*, July 29, 1932.
[9] *Frankfurter Zeitung und Handelsblatt, Börsen und Wirtschafts Kalender,
Wirtschaftschronik 1932*, pp. 9-10; James (1986, p. 355).
[10] "Government Not Expected to Take Action on Private Debts Until Meeting of
Foreign Creditor and German Debtor Committees," *The New York Times*, October 18,
1933.

refused to resolve the financial crisis of the municipalities, and these began to renege on their foreign debt-service payments.[11] Next, firms associated with Jewish capital, mainly department stores and banks harassed by the SA (Sturm Abteilung) during the first half of 1933, suspended debt-service payments (Einzig, 1934, p. 25). It is thus evident that, apart from the general foreign-exchange crisis with which the Reichsbank was faced, individual German debtors lacked the means with which to meet their obligations.

The Course of Default

This situation continued during the first six months of Hitler's chancellorship. The government, in particular Alfred Hugenberg, the Nazi ally who was economics minister during this period, hoped that the forthcoming World Economic Conference would resolve the debt issue. It was only after the conference failed that partial default became effective on July 1, 1993 (Dengg, 1986, pp. 363-364). Hjalmar Schacht, who had returned to the presidency of the Reichsbank, decided that only 50 percent of the debt service would be paid in foreign currency and the remainder would be paid in RM scrip, which the Reichsbank would repurchase at 50 percent of its face value. German debt-service payments were thus cut to 75 percent (James, 1986, pp. 403-405).

A further change in the arrangements was instituted when, after the inconclusive Berlin (Creditors') Conference of May 1934, the Reichsbank created the funding-bond scheme. The funding bonds were somewhat like the exit bonds issued by Mexico and other countries in the 1980s. A creditor accepting them in exchange for existing claims on Germany agreed to opt out of any future negotiations on the resumption of debt service. Although the principal was not reduced, interest payments were cut to 3 percent (Harris, 1935, pp. 57-58). These arrangements were eventually accepted by the creditors, although the Americans did not accept them until late 1935, because certain provisions of the funding-bond scheme involved discriminatory treatment of interest payments on the Dawes and Young loans.

These arrangements remained in force until the war, against the background of an increasingly autarkic economic regime, the evolution of which has been extensively chronicled elsewhere (Temin, 1991, provides the most recent account). By way of general background, it

---

[11] "Finance Minister von Krosigk Says Government Will Not Aid Cities on Debts," *The New York Times*, January 14, 1933; American Council of Foreign Bondholders, Newsletter 24, March 21, 1933.

should be noted that the first landmark in the development of the Nazi economy was Schacht's New Plan, introduced in September 1934. The plan set up twenty-five centers to allocate foreign exchange and regulate imports. After Schacht's defeat in the power struggle of 1936, a Four Year Plan, bearing more than a family resemblance to Soviet methods, was introduced under Hermann Göring's control. An increasingly large proportion of German trade was carried out under bilateral clearing agreements (Neal, 1979), but the treatment of the foreign debt was not changed.

Table 5 shows that all this had a drastic effect on the size of the debt, which fell by RM 6.6 billion between February 24, 1932 and September 30, 1934. Because German debt was denominated in the creditors' currencies, RM 6 billion of the recorded reduction was the result of the British and American devaluations and of the German determination not to follow suit but rather to maintain rigid exchange controls (Bonnell, 1940, p. 117). Later, the Finance Ministry calculated that the collapse of the Gold Bloc in 1936 had reduced the debt by another RM 1 billion, or 8.3 percent.[12] As Schuker (1988, p. 72, n. 63) has already pointed out, these figures suggest that the buybacks amounted to about RM 640 million at face value through mid-1934, an amount much smaller than claimed at the time by bondholders and interested governments.[13] I attempt to resolve this issue later by using confidential German figures on the buybacks themselves. These will show that the official figures understate the extent of the buybacks.

German Debt-Reduction Methods

Open-Market Bond Buybacks. German firms began to buy bonds on their own initiative no later than April 1932, and these purchases were regularized by an official process in July of that year.[14] The German authorities claimed that the repurchases had been discontinued before the debt negotiations in the spring of 1934 and that they were not resumed thereafter. In fact, buybacks had already become integral to

[12] BAK R2/232 (Handakten Könning), "Die Abwertung und ihre Folgen," February 24, 1936.

[13] But Schuker neglects the fact that the value of many bonds was protected by "gold clauses." The Germans listed $745 million of such bonds (AA Ha Pol, Anleihen und Wertpapiere, Anmeldstelle für Auslandsschulden, "Auf laufende deutsche Auslandsschulden," June 3, 1936). It is not possible to determine the extent to which the official published statistics reflect the fact that the face values of certain bonds were linked to gold and thus did not reflect the change in the dollar price of gold made by the Roosevelt administration.

[14] BAK R7/4706, "Circular No. 21852/32," July 27, 1932.

11

TABLE 5

GERMAN EXTERNAL DEBT, EXCLUDING REPARATIONS

(*in billions of reichsmarks*)

Date	Long-Term	Short-Term Standstill	Short-Term Other	Total Short-Term	Total
June 30, 1930	10.8	—	16.0	16.0	26.8
July 31, 1931	10.7	6.3	6.8	13.1	23.8
Nov. 30, 1931	10.7	5.4	5.2	10.6	21.3
Feb. 29, 1932	10.5	5.0	5.1	10.1	20.5
Sept. 30, 1932	10.2	4.3	5.0	9.3	19.5
Feb. 28, 1933	10.3	4.1	4.6	8.7	19.0
Sept. 30, 1933	7.4	3.0	4.4	7.4	14.8
Sept. 30, 1934	7.2	2.6	4.1	6.7	13.9
Sept. 30, 1935	6 .4	2.1	4.6	6.7	13.1
Sept. 30, 1936	6 .1	1.7	4.6	6.3	12.4
Sept. 30, 1937	5 .4	1.2	4.2	5.4	10.8
Sept. 30, 1938	5 .0	0.9	4.1	5.0	10.0
Sept. 30, 1939	4 .6	0.8	4.1	4.9	9.5

SOURCE: League of Nations, *Balance of Payments Statistics.*

the economic management of the Third Reich and were to remain an aspect of it until the last years of the war. Thus, the New Plan of September 1934 envisaged large buybacks of funding bonds; for the first year of the plan, RM 120 million worth of foreign exchange was allocated for the purchase of bonds having a face value of RM 216 million.[15] It seems that a shortage of reserves cut short this plan in early 1935; nevertheless, by May 1936, the U.S. Commerce Department concluded that repurchases of funding bonds had become an ongoing practice, a practice that, in fact, continued through 1939.[16] After the Anschluss, the policy was extended first to Austrian and then to Sudeten debts. In November 1938, the American ambassador complained that "various German dollar bonds selling in the American market at extremely low prices because of lack of payments continue to be repatriated by German foreign exchange made available for that

[15] BAK R2/227 (Handakten Könning), Copy of "Finanzierung der Ausfuhrförderung," August 16, 1934; "Zu der Denkschrift 'Neuregelung der Aussenhandels,'" n.d.

[16] R2/14216, "Uberlegungen zum Ausfuhrförderungsproblem" (p. 3), n.d.; AA Ha Pol, Anleihen und Wertpapiere (USA), Finanzwesen 2, "Behandlung der Dollar Funding-Bonds der Konversionskasse," April 2 and August 7, 1939; NA RG151, "Finance and Investments: Germany," May 6, 1936.

purpose."[17] The conquests of 1940 greatly enlarged the scope of these operations, although no information has been found on their extent; thus, repurchases of French loans were planned by the occupiers from 1940 to 1943. So great was the attachment of the German authorities to this practice that repurchases of Austrian loans continued until 1944.[18]

All previous writers have treated the mechanism by which buybacks were effected as part of the overall system for controlling foreign trade; in particular, they have regarded buybacks as part of the *zusatzausfuhr* ("additional export") procedures.[19] As these have been described in detail elsewhere (for example, Childs, 1958, chap. 5), I shall explain them relatively briefly.

As a result of the overvaluation of the reichsmark after the British and American devaluations, many German exporters could sell to the United Kingdom and United States only at a loss. A German exporter, however, could purchase bonds in New York with dollars earned from a trade transaction and resell the bonds in Germany, where he could make a substantial mark profit because of the large difference between bond prices in New York and Berlin. Figure 1 shows that the price difference varied between 25 and 40 percent for a particular class of bonds.

The procedure worked as follows: a German firm was permitted to use the proceeds of export sales to buy German securities in foreign markets if the firm could demonstrate that it could not otherwise make a profitable export sale. The firm was required to submit exact information on the prices being charged by foreign competitors in foreign markets and on the firm's own production costs. If these established that the firm could meet the foreign competition only at a loss, the

[17] AA Ha Pol, Finanzwesen 3, Finanzielle Beziehungen zwischen Deutschland und den Vereinigten Staaten, "Bedienung der amerikanischen Tranche der österreichen Anleihen," July 12, 1938.

[18] BAK R2/3698-3699, "File on the Repurchase of Austrian Bonds," 1944.

[19] The exception is Schuker (1988), who does not even mention the additional export arrangements. The most recent accounts by Doering (1969) and James (1986) treat the buybacks as part of the trade issue and not of the debt problem. This is misleading because "bond repatriation" was a major bone of contention between the Germans and the creditors. Thus, we read the complaint in the initial statement by the Creditors' Committee that, "apart from the advantage derived from failure to make full payment of interest on foreign loans, Germany is obtaining additional advantage from the ability to repurchase its obligations at important discounts" (Dulles Papers, Box 13, Berlin Conference File, "Statement of the Creditors' Committee," from the "Report of Pierre Jay, Laird Bell, and W.W. Cumberland on the German Debt Conference of April-May 1934," April 14, 1934.

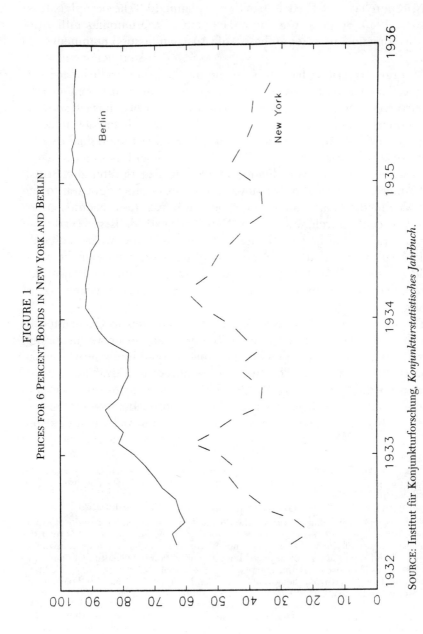

FIGURE 1

PRICES FOR 6 PERCENT BONDS IN NEW YORK AND BERLIN

SOURCE: Institut für Konjunkturforschung, *Konjunkturstatistisches Jahrbuch*.

firm could buy German bonds with that fraction of its export receipts that would, when the securities were resold in Germany, make the whole transaction profitable (Childs, 1958, pp. 36-37).

To facilitate the use of bond purchases for promoting additional exports, the Economics Ministry and Reichsbank issued regulations for the conversion of dollar bonds into mark-denominated bonds on which the original issuers would pay interest to the German firm or individual who had bought the bonds in New York (Zimmerman, 1933). This arrangement was not introduced until January 1934, however, when free trading of repurchased bonds was permitted on the Berlin stock market. Until then, the bonds could only be sold to the original issuers.

The decision to permit this sort of trading has an important implication. The prices at which debtors had been willing to repurchase their own bonds from a German who bought them in New York were considerably lower than those at which the bonds they had issued in Germany traded on the stock market. This indicates that, until 1934, the German authorities regarded buybacks as a way of favoring the efforts of debtor institutions to reduce their debt burdens.[20] After January 1934, however, with the institution of trading in Berlin, the buybacks became straightforward arbitrage operations, in which buyers exploited the difference between the prices on the New York and Berlin stock exchanges. The bonds were repatriated to Germany, but this did not reduce the debt burden of the German debtor company, which simply exchanged American for German creditors.

The buybacks were more than a covert export subsidy. The German authorities were at pains to claim publicly that "the purchase of these bonds takes place exclusively with foreign exchange received out of additional exports," and the negotiator for the American bondholders, John Foster Dulles, concluded that "no one not in the confidence of the Reichsbank can tell whether certain purchases are permitted which do not tie up with 'supplemental exports.'"[21] In fact, there exists confidential evidence that such purchases were permitted, but the various intelligence operations of the creditors and their secret informants

[20] NA RG59 862.51/3812, "Memorandum on Trading in Converted Dollar Bonds, Appendix B," February 27, 1934. Free trading of dollar bonds issued by German debtors was permitted if the bonds had been purchased by a German national before November 11, 1931.

[21] "The Repurchase of German Foreign Bonds," copy of a memorandum in BAK R2/227 (Handakten Könning), prepared in English by the German government, n.d.; Dulles Papers, Box 12, "Report by Laird Bell and John Foster Dulles to the Foreign Bondholders Protective Council on the German Dollar-Bond Situation and German Debt Conference of January 1934" (p. 19), February 13, 1934.

were unable to discover it at the time.[22] In November 1933, Finance Minister Lutz Graf Schwerin von Krosigk tried to obtain $21 million to repurchase a tranche of the 1930 Young loan, which was part of the public foreign debt; the Reichsbank was willing to make only $10 million available. At the same time, a company from Braunschweig was told that foreign currency might be made available for it to buy back part of its debt that bore a particularly heavy interest burden.[23] The contrast between the two cases is striking, as is the fact that no intermediation by an exporter was involved in either case. Clearly, buybacks were also performed directly by debtor companies.

It is thus proper to conclude that the additional export procedures making use of buybacks were originally aimed expressly at both export promotion and debt reduction, and this continued to be the case during 1934. When the industrialists' organization, the Reichsstand für Deutschen Industrie, urged that the bond transactions be replaced by a straight export subsidy, it was told by the authorities that the former were too important to be discontinued.[24] Even under the Four Year Plan in 1938-39, the Economics Ministry stated explicitly that buybacks were carried out to reduce the capital sum of the debt.[25] The policy differed after 1934 in that it was aimed only at reducing the national foreign indebtedness of Germany, not that of individual debtors.

Enter Colonel Norris. In the autumn of 1933, the course of the buybacks took a bizarre twist, one that would have had mere curiosity value if the financial dimensions of the affair had not been so large that they bear on our interpretation of the data. The financial press began to report the buyback operations in European markets of Lt. Col. Francis Norris, a retired British army officer with German connections and some shadowy associates.[26] The popular press took up the story and dwelt on the exploits of this "Colonel Lawrence of finance" and his expensive

[22] There are various coded messages and references to informants in the Federal Reserve Bank of New York's German telegrams file and in the Dulles Papers.

[23] BAK R2/4058, "Reichsbank Directorium to von Krosigk," November 15, 1933; "Letter to Miag Muhlenbau und Industrie Gesellschaft," November 25, 1933. See also NA 861.52/3683, "Report of the American Consul in Stuttgart to the Secretary of State," December 13, 1933.

[24] BAK R7/4711, "Letter to the Reichsstand für Deutschen Industrie," April 1, 1934; R2/14214, "Letter of May 30, 1934."

[25] BAK R7/3411, "Report on German Foreign Economic Relations [in 1938]," in section on "Transferpolitik" (p. 83), n.d.

[26] See "Colonel Lawrence of Finance, Buying, Buying, Buying. . . . His Movements Are Puzzling Four Capitals," *Sunday Dispatch*, April 5, 1934; "Light on Great Financial Mystery," *News Chronicle*, April 25, 1934.

16

mistress in the Avenue Foch. The British and French authorities, however, were concerned about the mysterious sources of Norris's money and his ability to offer prices above the going market prices for German issues. He therefore received the attentions of Scotland Yard and the French Sûreté.[27]

The Reichsbank denied all knowledge of Norris's operations, and the whole truth did not come out until a year after his arrest for fraud by the French in May 1934.[28] Norris had been fronting for an operation run by Joseph Goebbels to raise money for the Nazi party through buybacks of German bonds. Goebbels's position gave Norris easy access to the foreign exchange needed for the repurchases, and the party coffers were then enriched by the resales in Germany.[29] The dimensions of the Norris affair were enormous. Hilger von Scherpenberg, Schacht's nephew and informal link to the city of London, informed the Bank of England that as much as RM 300 million had been spent on the Colonel's operations.[30] At average market prices for 1934, this sum represents the repurchase of bonds having a face value of RM 550 million.

Repurchases of Scrip and Blocked Marks. Attempts were made to use repurchases of scrip and blocked marks as part of the additional export system, thus combining export subsidies and debt reduction, as with bond repurchases. From the start of Schacht's moratorium on foreign-exchange payments in July 1933, it was the German intention to create a secondary market in these instruments and to use it for debt repurchases.[31] Records of these transactions exist until 1941.[32]

The use of scrip began in June 1933, when it was declared that 50 percent of interest payments would be made in this form. The scheme allowed foreign importers to pay for German exports in German scrip, purchased at a discount on the secondary market and valued at that

[27] Bank of England, OV34/84, "Rowe-Dutton to Layton," March 19, 1934; "Minute by Pinsent," April 25, 1934; OV34/85, "Summary of Articles by *De Telegraaf's* Correspondent in Paris," n.d.

[28] Bank of England, OV34/84, "Reichsbank Directorium to the Bank of England," December 29, 1933.

[29] Bank of England, OV34/85,"Colonel Norris [Siepmann Memorandum]," March 11, 1936.

[30] Bank of England, OV34/84, "Note of a Conversation with von Scherpenberg Held on May 23, 1934."

[31] DGFP, Series C, Vol. 1, No. 211, "Circular of the Foreign Ministry Circulated by Karl Ritter, Head of the Foreign Ministry Economic Department, to All German Legations," May 5, 1933.

[32] BAK R2/31032-31034, 14217; R7/3629, "Balance-of-Payments Accounts for 1938, 1939, and 1941."

discount when used to pay for German exports. If scrip sold at a discount of 50 percent in New York, for example, an American importer wishing to purchase $10,000 worth of German goods would pay the German exporter with scrip the face value of which was $20,000. The profit to the exporter, however, would be less than the $10,000 difference, because the scrip acquired in this way would only be converted into reichsmarks by the Reichsbank at a rate above the official exchange rate. The Reichsbank thus captured some of the mark profits on the transaction.

A large secondary market also existed in the blocked marks used to pay interest on the short-term standstill debts and, from June 1933, to amortize the long-term debt (Ellis, 1941, p. 199; James, 1986, p. 392). German exports could also be bought with blocked marks, which, in 1934, for example, could be purchased by the foreign importer at discounts ranging between 30 and 60 percent, depending on the type of blocked mark involved.[33]

Proposals for Comprehensive Debt Reduction. Schacht always claimed that he desired a comprehensive debt-conversion operation and that he was driven to continue the buybacks because the creditors could not agree among themselves on any comprehensive scheme.[34] The German authorities devoted much ingenuity to debt-reducing devices, in addition to the funding-bond scheme and the repurchases of scrip and blocked marks. These included the clearing agreements with Britain, Switzerland, and Holland, which were to some extent forced on Germany (see Chapter 4 below), and unilateral actions, particularly against U.S. creditors, who were made to accept lower interest rates on the reparation-related Dawes and Young loans. Once the funding bonds had been issued, moreover, the Germans offered to repurchase them at 40 percent of face value, an offer no creditors took up.[35] Most novel and bizarre of all, however, was the debt-for-Jews swap proposed by Schacht to the British in the spring of 1938. As described by Barkai (1989), the financing of Jewish emigration was integrated into the blocked-mark system during the period of the New Plan. This

---

[33] Ellis (1941, p. 397) The categories of blocked marks differed depending on whether they originated from amortization of the long-term debt, interest on the short-term debt, or profits from foreign investments in Germany. The uses to which the blocked marks could be put differed according to the specific regulations, and this led to the differences in the discounts.

[34] FRBNY, German Country File, "Memorandum of Harpen for Governor Harrison," July 4, 1933.

[35] *Frankfurter Zeitung und Handelsblatt, Börsen und Wirtschafts Kalender 1935*, p. 67.

policy culminated in an attempt by Schacht to negotiate the emigration of 400,000 Jews in return for their agreement to relinquish their assets to the German government (Barkai, 1989, pp. 144-145). An additional proposal was that the emigration of 150,000 German and Austrian Jews would be facilitated if world Jewry would liquidate Germany's debts. This unpleasant episode is an index of Germany's desire to use all means at its disposal to achieve debt reduction.[36]

How Much Was Bought Back?

Earlier scholarly accounts of the buybacks all accepted the claim of the German authorities that no bonds were repurchased after November 1933 and that the total amount repurchased from the beginning of 1932 was RM 781 million (Harris, 1935, p. 38; Bonnell, 1940, p. 56; Ellis, 1941, p. 300). Yet, creditors privately suspected that the amounts were considerably larger; at the Berlin Conference in May 1934, their representatives cited German statistics indicating that over RM 500 million had been allocated for repurchases in the previous nine months alone, an amount that pointed to much larger figures at prevailing market discounts.[37]

The German statements were false, and German negotiators were instructed to hold back the figures on repurchases until creditor pressure for information became intense. Later, Schacht told Hitler and the cabinet that "the bond buyback in 1933 amounted to over RM 1 milliard" (that is, an American billion).[38] This statement clearly contradicts the official German position and also contradicts the conclusion by Schuker (1988, p. 72) that, once allowance is made for the effects of the dollar devaluation, the published German statistics imply that only RM 620 million were bought back in 1933-34. Table 6 attempts to resolve the issue by using confidential German statistics in place of the published figures, which are unreliable. The sources and methods used to construct the table are described in Appendix A but deserve brief mention here.

[36] AA Ha Pol, Anleihen und Wertpapiere, "Wiehl Telegram," December 12, 1938, and "Dirksen Telegram," December 16, 1938. Dirksen's telegram refers to Schacht's discussion with British government members about financing Jewish emigration through loans from "World Jewry"; a long note in the margin of the Wiehl telegram describes a proposal to finance Jewish emigration through an agreed upon write-off of Germany's external debt.

[37] Dulles Papers, Box 13, Berlin Conference File, "Statement of the Creditors' Committee," from the "Report of Pierre Jay, Laird Bell, and W.W. Cumberland on the German Debt Conference of April-May 1934," Annex 8, May 2, 1934.

[38] AA SW, Finanzwesen 2, "Meeting at the Reichsbank of January 25, 1934"; BAK R43II/783, "Meeting of the Heads of Departments on June 7, 1934."

Precise figures for expenditures on buybacks can be found for the period from 1935 to 1941 in the balance-of-payments and export-subsidy statistics, and the amounts bought back can then be derived by applying the appropriate secondary-market discounts. (Unfortunately, no break-down has been found for 1936-37 that would permit the separation of bond repurchases from scrip and blocked-mark repurchases; the figures in the table therefore use the proportions obtaining in 1935.) Annual data can likewise be obtained for 1933 and 1934 but must be estimated for 1932, when many of the bond buybacks reportedly took place. The estimate is based on a 1936 benchmark computed from German figures (which are consistent with U.S. estimates for bond buybacks).[39]

TABLE 6

REPURCHASES OF BONDS, SCRIP, AND BLOCKED
MARKS, 1932-1939
(*in millions of reichsmarks*)

Year	Bonds	Scrip & Blocked Marks
1932	859	n.a.
1933	1,181	—
1934	489	91
1935	77	462
1936	29	268
1937	18	131
1938	46	142
1939	37	191
1940	—	59
1941	13	25

SOURCES: BAK R2/31032-31034, 14217 (1934-1937); R7/3529, R7/3068 (1938-1941), R7/4572 (1932-1933). See Appendix A for details.

A figure that suggests the extent of the buybacks comes from the Reich Office for the Registration of Foreign Debts. It shows that 35 percent of all dollar-denominated bonds were in German possession by 1936; this figure does not cover most of the British, Swiss, and Dutch bonds, which were chiefly denominated in those countries' currencies,

[39] I am indebted to Albrecht Ritschl for pointing out an error in my original calcula-tions for 1938-39. See Ritschl (1991) for a thorough analysis of the balance-of-payments accounts for those years.

or repurchases of agricultural mortgages reported by German officials.[40] A related source of information is a survey carried out by the *Frankfurter Zeitung* in 1934, which I shall use extensively later in my empirical analysis. This survey gives the amounts outstanding in mid-1932 and mid-1934 of 121 German bonds issued in the United States. The amounts bought back between those dates can be calculated by subtracting the amounts due to be amortized (obtained from Kuczynski, 1928) from the change in the amounts outstanding.[41] This calculation shows that repurchases totaled 32 percent of the face value of the bonds surveyed. The most comprehensive figure, and the one I have used to construct Table 6, derives from an estimate by the U.S. commercial attaché, who used company balance sheets and calculated that 40 percent of the industrial bonds had been bought back by the end of 1936.[42] In addition, he judged that 30 percent of the mortgage bonds, 20 percent of the municipal bonds, and 10 percent of other bonds had been repurchased, which, on a weighted-average calculation, implies that 32 percent of the total debt had been repurchased. Applying this percentage to the 1931 debt stock adjusted for the effects of the U.K. and U.S. devaluations, I conclude that RM 2,635 million of bonds had been repurchased by the end of 1936. The figure for 1932 in Table 6 is obtained by deducting the annual estimates for the period from 1933 to 1936. The large size of that figure may reflect buybacks that reputedly took place in the 1920s.[43]

The buybacks recorded for 1934 should be laid at Colonel Norris's door. At prevailing discounts, the RM 300 million spent (in London and Amsterdam) translate into repurchases of bonds having a face value of RM 550 million. Given that most of Norris's operations began in September 1933, attained a large scale in 1934, and terminated with his arrest in May 1934, one suspects that the RM 250 million recorded by German sources as having been allocated for buybacks in 1934

[40] AA Ha Pol, Finanzwesen 3, Finanzielle Beziehung von Deutschland mit den USA, Copy of "Deutsche Besitz in Dollarbonds," marked "Streng Geheim," November 29, 1936. Some dollar bonds issued in Holland are included in this table, which shows that $421.94 million at face value had been repurchased by 1937. An earlier document from the same source, dated June 3, 1936, put the face value of repurchased dollar-denominated debt at $393.66 million.

[41] *Frankfurter Zeitung und Handelsblatt, Börsen und Wirtschafts Kalender 1935*, p. 67.

[42] NA RG151 C 640, Germany, "German Indebtedness to the United States," January 7, 1937, where it is reported that 59.7 percent of the dollar bonds of the twenty-one largest industrial companies were still outstanding.

[43] NA RG59 862.51/3636, "Memorandum from the Office of the Economic Advisor [Herbert Feis]," May 1, 1933

relate solely to Norris's activities in European markets. This inference is corroborated by a survey of buybacks carried out by the New York Stock Exchange that records repurchases in the first half of 1934 of only $12 million at face value. This information is incomplete, however, because it refers only to those issues traded on the stock market and thus covers only 62 of the 132 German bonds issued in the United States. Nevertheless, there seems no reason to suppose that huge repurchases took place on the curb market or in free trading when they did not occur on the stock market.[44] We can safely conclude, therefore, that buybacks did not take place in the United States during 1934. This information will be useful later in interpreting my quantitative analysis.

The large size of the buybacks shown in Table 6 has two implications. These concern contemporary views about the size of the operation and the importance of the German episode in a broader historical and global perspective.

Dealing with these points in reverse order, I start by observing that this was by far the largest buyback operation ever. The Latin American bond buybacks in the 1930s studied by Jorgensen and Sachs (1989) amounted to only $120 million, compared with the $422 million repurchased by Germany from the United States alone down to the end of 1936. This was 35 percent of total German long-term debt to the United States. Only Peru repurchased a larger proportion of its debt, 47 percent, but the defaulted debt involved, $88 million, is tiny by comparison. All in all, 33 percent of the German total long-term debt was bought back, and a further 7 percent was reduced by purchases of scrip and blocked marks.[45] The German buybacks amounted to about 2.8 percent of global debt in 1932,[46] an unprecedented program by a single country when one considers that only 4.1 percent of global debt was repurchased in the 1980s by all the debtor countries involved and that much of that was done by negotiated buybacks (Bouchet and Hay, 1989).

[44] FRBNY, Committee on German Foreign Credits File, "Memorandum by J.M.B. Hoxsey for Richard Whitney, President of the New York Stock Exchange," August 3, 1934.

[45] Short-term obligations were serviced by payments into blocked "register" mark accounts. After the creation of the Konversionskasse für Auslandsschulden in July 1933, the Germans attempted the scrip-repurchase scheme described earlier, and some creditors retained scrip from this period. When the funding bonds were introduced, they were serviced by payments into blocked "conversion" mark accounts, but creditors could also accept payment in scrip (Bonnell, 1940, pp. 54-56). It is evident from the balance-of-payments accounts for 1938-39 (BAK R7/3629) that actual scrip repurchases were minimal.

[46] Estimated by the Royal Institute of International Affairs (1937, p. 222) to be £7,000 million ($34,020 million) for 1931.

Finally, Table 6 implies that the truth about the size of the German buybacks lies somewhere between the estimate by Feis, economic advisor to the U.S. State Department (NA 862.51/3636), that as much as $2,000 million had been repurchased in 1932, and the German official claims mentioned above. Feis's figure would be excessive for the whole period, let alone for 1932. Nevertheless, it is clear that the buybacks continued after 1933 and this, together with the large figure for 1933, means that they were much larger than has been stated in previous accounts, which have accepted German published statistics at face value.

Finally, the high tide of buybacks took place before Schacht took over the Economics Ministry in the summer of 1934, which shows that the buybacks were not specifically a "Schachtian devilry," as Harrod (1951) once called them.

3 WHO BENEFITED FROM THE BUYBACKS?

The Bulow-Rogoff Case against Buybacks

A strong and influential case against buybacks originates with Bulow and Rogoff (1988). Take the simplest example of a country that owes $1 billion but will be able to pay only $100 million. The market price of its debt will be 10 cents. The debtor country cannot benefit from a repurchase that knocks its debt down to $500 million, because the price of the remaining debt will rise to 20 cents, and the country will have spent $50 million without any reduction in its debt burden (Bulow and Rogoff, 1990, p. 33). It has been argued that something like this occurred in the case of Bolivia in 1988, when the face value of Bolivian debt was almost halved by a buyback but the market value fell by only 1 percent. A buyback cannot be beneficial to the debtor unless there is some positive probability that the debtor will repay in full, so that the cost of the buyback is offset by potential savings on expected future debt service.

Yet the debtor may not gain from a buyback even when this condition is satisfied. For a $1 reduction in consumption, the debtor can retire $1/p$ units of debt at face value, where p is the average secondary-market price of its debt. This reduces the expected payment on a unit of debt by $(1 - G)/p$, where $1 - G$ is the probability that the debt will be repaid in full. But $1 - G$ is also the marginal value of the debt; it measures the creditors' expected receipts from the addition of an extra unit of debt. Clearly, the debtor cannot gain unless the reduction in future debt payments exceeds the $1 used in the buyback, which means that $(1 - G)/p$ must be less than 1. But $1 - G$ will be less than p, because the latter includes not just expected future debt service but also the creditors' compensation in the event of a partial or total default, which is usually taken to be the value of the assets seized from the debtor and shared on a *pro rata* basis among the creditors. Appendix B shows this explicitly in the context of a very simple model. Claessens and Diwan (1989) provide a more complicated model that explicitly includes investment.

To forestall an argument often made in answer to this reasoning, it should be pointed out that the reasoning continues to hold even when the buyback has output-enhancing effects.[47] When a debtor country is on the "wrong side" of the so-called Debt Laffer Curve, the case emphasized by Krugman (1989), the marginal value of its debt is negative, which only strengthens the argument against a buyback in the Bulow-Rogoff framework, as Bulow and Rogoff (1988, 1991) have pointed out.

A corollary of this analysis is that the price of the remaining debt must rise to reflect the gains that the remaining creditors make from the buyback: the buyback must reduce the market value of the debt by less than it reduces the face value. As the debtor has paid $1/p$ and gained only $(1 - G)/p$, the remaining $1 - (1 - G)/p$ must go to the creditors, and, because the buyback has reduced the face value of the debt, their gains must be expressed as an increase in the market value of the remaining debt, achieved by an increase in the average price.

This result, whereby the effect of a buyback is merely a transfer from the debtor to the creditors, must be modified when the buyback is financed by reducing reserves, a proportion of which may be seized in the event of a default (Bulow and Rogoff, 1988). If this default penalty is q, the creditors pay for qG of the buyback, as G is the probability of default. From each dollar of reserves spent on the buyback, then, the debtor saves the expected value of the portion that might be seized in the event of a default, and the cost of repurchasing $\$1/p$ of debt becomes $1 - qG$. Therefore, Bulow and Rogoff argue that a repurchase hurts the debtor whenever $1 - qG > (1 - G)/p$. This will be cited below as the Bulow-Rogoff criterion.

How the Market Value of the German Debt Changed

At first sight, the evidence seems to say that something very similar to the Bolivian experience occurred in the German case. The total market value of German debt to the United States was $374 million in April 1932.[48] Assuming that all of the debt recorded by the Anmeldstelle für Auslandsschulden as having been repurchased before 1936 was in fact repurchased by August 1934, before the New Plan came into operation, the market value of German debt to the United States

---

[47] As was mentioned in the introduction, this may be true when a severe debt overhang exists—when the negative transfer of resources to the creditors reduces the amount of savings available for investment and growth, and the prospect of repeated rescheduling weakens the incentive of the debtor to make painful efforts to grow out of the crisis (Claessens and Diwan, 1989, p. 263). The simplest case in which this argument cannot be accepted for a buyback is one in which the rate of return on the reserves to repurchase debt exceeds the return on alternative domestic investments (Kenen, 1991).

[48] The market prices used are those of the Institut für Konjunkturforschung (1936).

would have been $361 million in August 1934, only slightly less than it was in April 1932.[49] August 1934 is one of the appropriate dates to use for this comparison, as secondary-market prices were probably influenced thereafter by the institutions created by the New Plan and the terms offered to creditors under the funding-bond scheme. There is, however, another appropriate date to use: December 1933. This is appropriate because the Norris-Goebbels operation, which involved only European bonds, can account for the entire RM 250 million allocated for buybacks in 1934, which implies that repurchases did not occur in the United States in 1934. When the debt remaining in the United States after repurchase is valued at the December 1933 price, the market value is $363 million, which is again quite close to the April 1932 figure.

Similar results can be obtained in yet another way. The most precise information concerning the reduction in the amount of debt outstanding can be obtained from data collected by the *Frankfurter Zeitung* on the circulation of German bonds in the United States down to August 1934. These data were obtained from a survey of German debtors and appeared in the *Börsen und Wirtschafts Kalender* published by the newspaper in 1935.[50] They include information on 116 of the 132 German bonds issued between 1924 and 1932. The reduction in the amount of each issue outstanding can be found by subtracting the amount outstanding in the 1934 survey from that recorded in the yearbook's survey for July 1932. Table 7 provides information on the market value of those bonds during the large buybacks from 1932 to 1934. Evaluated at the average market price in New York for all German bonds, the value of these bonds in April 1932 was $345 million; in August 1934, the value was $385 million. When, instead, the issues are valued at their individual market prices for April 1932 and December 1933, their value rises from $254 million to $413 million—a strong "Debt Laffer Curve effect." Unfortunately, I have not been able

---

[49] AA Ha Pol, Anleihen und Wertpapiere, Anmeldstelle für Auslandsschulden, "Auf laufende deutsche Auslandsschulden," June 3, 1936.

[50] An earlier working paper, (Klug, 1992), relied on buyback data collected by the New York Stock Exchange in 1934 (FRBNY, Committee on German Foreign Credits File, "Memorandum by J.M.B. Hoxsey for Richard Whitney, President of the New York Stock Exchange," August 3, 1934.). These data cover 62 issues, 44 of which are recorded as having been partly repurchased. Close inspection of these figures, however, suggests that they reflect buybacks of 13 issues before 1932, carried out as part of the amortization of those issues. I am therefore using an alternative data set here. The two sets of data do not yield different results, however, about the effects of buybacks on market value.

TABLE 7

CHANGES IN THE MARKET VALUE OF GERMAN BONDS IN THE
UNITED STATES, 1932-1934
(*in million of dollars*)

	June 1932	January 1934
116 long-term bonds:		
Valued at average market price	345	385
Valued at individual prices	254	413
	April 1932	August 1934
Total long-term debt	374	361
40 partly repurchased issues:		
Valued at average market price	225	222
Valued at individual prices	185	224

to find price information for all of these bonds individually for 1934.
Prices are available only for those 44 issues that were traded on the
New York Stock Exchange. The value of the 44 issues, all of which
were partly repurchased, changed only slightly, from $225.5 million in
1932 to $222.2 million in 1934. The change in the market value of
these issues can also be calculated by valuing each bond at its own
individual price. Prices for August 1934 are not available for all of the
issues (indeed, they seem to be completely unavailable for some
issues), but, working with those issues for which prices are available in
months close to April 1931 and August 1934, one finds that the market
value of 40 partly repurchased bonds rose from $185.8 million to
$223.8 million.[51] Thus, it appears that the buybacks may actually have
raised the market value of the debt and certainly did not reduce it.

This result cannot be attributed to parallel developments in the U.S.
bond market. Although prices for long-term bonds rose during this
period, the increase was only 2 to 5 percent for the bonds listed by
Homer and Sylla (1989, table 48, p. 253). German prices in New York,
by contrast, are shown in Figure 2 to have fluctuated wildly but to
have been 40 percent above their lowest 1932 level at the end of 1934.

These calculations appear to offer strong support for the predictions
of the Bulow-Rogoff model. Indeed, some of them imply that Germany

[51] Bond prices were taken from the *Commercial and Financial Chronicle*, the *Fitch
Bond Book* for 1935, and the Foreign Bondholders Protective Council *Annual Report* for
1936.

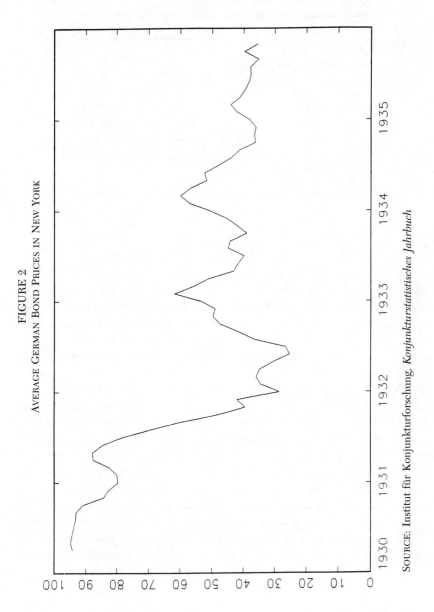

FIGURE 2

AVERAGE GERMAN BOND PRICES IN NEW YORK

SOURCE: Institut für Konjunkturforschung, *Konjunkturstatistisches Jahrbuch*

was on the "wrong side" of the Debt Laffer Curve, where the marginal price of the debt is negative, a situation that only strengthens the case against buybacks in the Bulow-Rogoff framework.

Testing the Bulow-Rogoff Model

It might be argued that the market value of the debt rose for other reasons; for example, the expectation of a debt settlement during the negotiations from January through May 1934 was thought to have driven up prices during that period (Harris, 1935, pp. 56-57). It is thus necessary to see whether there is a statistically significant relation between the amount repurchased and the change in the market value of a bond issue. Doing so directly tests the predictions of the Bulow-Rogoff model and the stronger proposition that Germany was on the "wrong side" of the Debt Laffer Curve.

As already mentioned, the data contained in the *Frankfurter Zeitung's Börsen und Wirtschafts Kalender* for 1935 can be used for this purpose. For 96 of the bonds involved, Kuczynski (1928) provides amortization schedules for 1932 and 1933. The amount of each bond bought back can thus be calculated by subtracting the amount amortized from the difference between the face value of an issue in June 1932 and its value in mid-1934. (In cases in which principal was due to be repaid during the transfer moratorium in the second half of 1933, the scheduled payments were excluded from the calculation.) The percentage changes in the market values of the individual issues can then be regressed on the percentages of the face values of those issues that were bought back.

This cross-sectional approach using individual bonds is an appropriate test of the Bulow-Rogoff prediction and is fully analogous to the cross-sectional approach using individual countries for the 1980s. Three considerations support this analogy. First, and most important, many of the debtor companies and institutions were, as we have seen, threatened with bankruptcy and liable to default on their loans. The individual issuers thus faced a potential, and in some cases actual, debt-service constraint, with their own positive probabilities of default. Second, the creditors threatened to confiscate the assets of each German debtor separately, which is equivalent to the threat against a sovereign debtor in the Bulow-Rogoff framework. The specific threat employed was to seize the U.S. assets of the company if its bonds were in default. In the case of a debtor having no such assets, action was threatened against the

U.S. assets of the German banks with which the debtor had deposits.[52] It is thus apparent that each individual issue had a particular default cost associated with it (that is, the q of the Bulow-Rogoff criterion). The important point here is that the threat involved the seizure of some part of the assets of the German companies, as in the Bulow-Rogoff model, not all of their assets, as would be the case with an ordinary corporate bankruptcy. Third, the buybacks directly reduced the indebtedness of the individual issuers until January 1934, when it became possible to trade repurchased bonds on the Berlin stock exchange. I have already shown, however, that there were no significant buybacks in the United States during 1934. Although the *Frankfurter Zeitung*'s survey dates from mid-1934, the data can be regarded as referring to a period in which the amount of an issue repurchased should have affected only the value of that particular issue rather than the value of German debt in general.

One caveat remains, however. In July 1933, the German government instituted a moratorium on the transfer of interest and principal. For part of the period covered by the data, then, the probability of complete repudiation depended not just on the decisions of the individual German issuers but also on those of the government and Reichsbank. Thus, factors specifically affecting the behavior of an individual issue may not be able to explain all of the change in its market value.

In August 1934, when all debts were consolidated into funding bonds controlled by the Konversionskasse, the German debt structure lost its special character, becoming similar to that of sovereign debtors in the 1980s. In fact, after June 1933, when the Reichsbank began to limit debt-service payments, each firm's payments became constrained by the government's decisions as well as its own.

Empirical Specification

In order to estimate the relation between the face value bought back and the change in market value, it is necessary to correct for a sample-selection problem caused by the fact that not all issues were repurchased. This is done here by jointly estimating the decision to repurchase part of a particular issue and the effect of the repurchase on the market value of that issue. The tobit two-stage least-squares method is used, following Maddala (1983, pp. 240-242). First, the amount repurchased is estimated as a function of a group of exogenous variables that characterize a

---

[52] DGFP, Series C, Vol. 1, No. 294, "Private and Confidential Aide-Memoire Attached to a Letter from Dulles to Schacht," June 3, 1933.

particular bond. Because certain bonds were not repurchased and were included in the sample, the parameters are estimated by the tobit method. Next, the change in the value of the bond is estimated as a function of the bond's characteristics and the fitted value of the amount repurchased (that is, the amount predicted at the first stage). Thus the model is

$$R = Z_1\beta_1 + \varepsilon_1 \ , \tag{1}$$

$$CV = \hat{R}\gamma + Z_2\beta_2 + \varepsilon_2 \ , \tag{2}$$

where $R = R^\circ$ if $R^\circ > 0$, and $R = 0$ otherwise. In these equations, R° is the amount of the bond bought back, calculated by subtracting contractual amortization from the reduction in the face value of the bond. This number is negative for some bonds, suggesting that they defaulted on contractual amortization, although we have actual knowledge of this for only three issues. The model is therefore censored, as these observations are excluded. Z_1 is a vector of bond characteristics, and ε_1 is a normally distributed error with mean zero. CV is the change in the market value of a repurchased issue between April 1932 and December 1933. Observations for which $R^\circ \leq 0$ are excluded. $\hat{R}$ is the amount of the bond repurchased as calculated for equation (1) and serves as an instrument for the actual amount repurchased. Z_2 is a vector of bond characteristics, with at least one less variable than β_1, used in equation (1), to identify the model.

Estimation of equation (2) by ordinary least squares leads to biased and inconsistent estimates unless a variable is included to account for the censoring of the sample. To overcome this problem, a generalization of Heckman's (1979) two-step estimator is employed. This generalization is derived by Vella (1993). First, we estimate equation (1) by maximum likelihood and obtain the generalized residuals from the regression. For the observations with $R > 0$, these are found by Vella to be simply $R - Z_1\beta_1$, which are similar to the least-squares residuals. The change in face value is then estimated by

$$CV = Z_2\beta_2 + \hat{R}\gamma_1 + \lambda\gamma_2 + \varepsilon_2 \ , \tag{3}$$

where λ is the selectivity term, which is equal to the generalized residuals in equation (1), $\gamma_2 = \sigma_{12}/\sigma_1$, which is the ratio of the covariance of the residuals in the two equations to the standard error of equation (1), and ε_2 is an error term with mean zero.

To derive unbiased and efficient estimates of equation (3), an appropriate correction must be made to the standard errors caused by inclusion of the selectivity term in (3). This is done by calculating the standard errors using the covariance matrices derived in appendix B of Vella (1989).

Estimation Results. Equations (1), (2), and (3) are used to investigate the relation between quantity of a bond repurchased and changes in the market price. When estimating equations (1) and (2), a number of bond characteristics were included in the vector Z_2: debt service in 1932-33 as a proportion of the principal, the yield of each issue, and the lowest price of each issue in 1932. Dummies divide the bonds by issue into municipalities, utilities, commercial and industrial firms, and other quasi-public financial institutions (that is, the Länder savings banks and the institutions supplying credit to agriculture). A stock variable indicates whether a bond was originally issued on the stock market, the curb market, or in what was termed "free trading."

The results of the tobit estimation are given in the first column of Table 8 and show that price and debt service, but not yield, are significant in explaining the proportion repurchased. The stock dummy is insignificant, which shows that there was no preference for repurchasing the bonds traded on the New York Stock Exchange, despite the fact that they were regarded as being of higher quality and received higher ratings from investors' services such as Moodys. Finally, the results indicate that repurchases were most likely to occur in two categories of bonds, those of private companies (represented by the "commercial" dummy) and those of the mortgage and agricultural banks (represented by the "quasi-public financial institutions" dummy).

The results of the second-stage regressions are shown in the second column of Table 8. The fitted quantity repurchased variable has a strong negative effect on the change in the market value of a bond. It is, indeed, impossible to reject (at the 99 percent level) the hypothesis that the coefficient on this buyback variable is greater absolutely than -1, whereas the Bulow-Rogoff model says that it should be smaller absolutely than -1. The constant term and coefficients for the bond characteristics are also large, however, which implies that the buybacks themselves must be large in order to conflict with the effect predicted by Bulow and Rogoff, that the value of the debt will change by an amount that offsets the buyback. For example, if 60 percent of a commercial bond is repurchased and its debt service is 5 percent of face value, the equation predicts that its market value will fall by only 40 percent. When the buyback is above 68 percent of face value, however, it reduces the market value of the debt by the full amount repurchased and can reduce it even more. Even so, it is impossible to

TABLE 8

DEBT BUYBACKS AND CHANGES IN MARKET VALUE

Dependent Variable	R	CV
Constant	6.6789	2.9733
	(4.423)	(4.583)
Price 32	−1.3400	—
	(2.301)	
Yield	0.2743	−0.2068
	(0.223)	(0.024)
Service	0.4812	−9.4375
	(2.194)	(3.876)
Commercial	3.5111	2.1134
	(4.342)	(3.574)
Utilities	1.0544	1.1459
	(1.532)	(3.460)
Quasi-public	2.3901	1.6827
financial institutions	(3.241)	(3.531)
Municipal	−8.3334	−1.0297
	(1.042)	(4.073)
Stock (New York)	−5.2134	−0.1110
	(1.255)	(0.671)
Fitted repurchases	—	−7.8398
		(4.454)
Generalized residuals	—	−0.2300
		(2.908)
R^2	—	0.44
$F(9,86)$	—	7.52

NOTE: t-statistics are in parentheses.

reject the hypotheses that the size of the constant term, any of the dummy-variable coefficients, and the coefficient on the proportion of the debt repurchased are jointly less than −1. Thus, a buyback reduces the market value of the debt by a percentage at least as large as the amount by which it reduces the face value.

The high value of the coefficient on fitted repurchases is disturbing. It suggests that the Germans succeeded in driving down the prices of those bonds that were heavily repurchased. They were, in fact, often accused of threatening repudiation in order to drive down the bond prices and thus reduce the cost of their buybacks.[53] For this to have been a successful strategy, however, the creditors would have had to believe that the threats of repudiation were more credible than they actually were. Another possibility is that the prices of the repurchased bonds continued to fall because creditors believed that the probabilities of default on those bonds were higher than the Germans knew them to be. The implications of such divergent perceptions concerning default are discussed later in this study.

Three conclusions follow from this exercise. First, the negative coefficient on the percentage of face value repurchased says that there is no evidence for a Debt Laffer Curve effect. Second, occurrences such as the Bolivian buyback of 1988, in which the market value remained unchanged after the repurchase, cannot be taken as evidence that a buyback causes market value to rise, as this happened to the value of the total German debt but not to the values of the bonds bought back. Third, the predictions of the Bulow-Rogoff model are not confirmed, because it is impossible to reject the hypothesis that the buyback reduces the market value of an issue by more than its face value.

The Marginal Value of the Debt

Light can be shed on whether Germany gained from the buybacks by trying to estimate the marginal value of the debt. If the marginal value is less than the average value, a debtor cannot benefit from a buyback within the Bulow-Rogoff framework. If the average and marginal values are equal, a debtor may gain from the buyback according to the Bulow-Rogoff criterion and will certainly not lose. Such a finding would not in itself reject the Bulow-Rogoff model, but I shall argue below, in conjunction with other findings, that it is possible to show not merely that Germany gained from the buybacks but that the model itself is not supported by the evidence.

The marginal value is found by estimating the elasticity of the secondary-market price with respect to the face value of the debt. As the market value of the debt is $pD = V$, where p is the secondary-market price and D is the face value, differentiating V with respect to D gives the marginal value, $p_m = p(1 - e)$, where p_m is the marginal value, and e is the elasticity of the average price with respect to the face value. If the elasticity can be shown to be zero, the average and marginal values must be equal and the case against the German buybacks does not hold.

---

[53] BAK R43II/787, "Telegram from the German Ambassador in London," June 23, 1934.

Attempts to estimate this relation for the 1980s (for example, Claessens, 1988; Cohen, 1989) had to rely on cross-country data, making it difficult to draw policy conclusions with regard to any individual country. The nature of the sample used here, however, makes it possible to estimate the marginal value of German debt from a cross section of individual bond issues in which, as before, each issue has its own default cost and thus serves as an observation in the same way that individual countries have served as observations in previous attempts to estimate the Debt Laffer Curve.

The results are recorded in Table 9, where $\log p$ is the logarithm of the price of an issue in 1932, and $\log d$ is the logarithm of its face value. The t-statistics were calculated from the heteroscedastic-consistent standard errors because the ordinary-least-squares estimates exhibited heteroscedasticity. The elasticity of the coefficient is of the expected sign but clearly close to zero and is insignificantly different from zero at a level above 50 percent.

Evidently, marginal and average values were equal, and Germany could not have lost from the buybacks. This is exactly the result one would expect in the light of the previous exercise, which showed that a buyback reduces market value by more than it reduces face value. It also conflicts with the basic Bulow-Rogoff framework, especially when

TABLE 9

DEBT-VALUATION EQUATION

Dependent Variable	Log p
Constant	−0.9933 (3.032)
Log d	0.0042 (0.137)
Service	0.0850 (3.110)
Yield	3.1679 (0.677)
Official	−0.1973 (3.071)
Commercial	0.0123 (0.162)
Quasi-public financial institutions	−0.0204 (0.287)
Stock	0.0427 (0.831)
Municipal	−0.3804 (6.511)
R^2	0.29
$F(8,88)$	4.52

NOTE: t-statistics are in parentheses.

35

the historical context is considered. Bulow and Rogoff (1988, 1991) claim that, in the context of their model, equality between marginal and average values implies that lenders expect an all-or-nothing payout.[54] This finding is hard to reconcile with the fact that partial debt-service payments were made both before the transfer moratorium of July 1933 and after the introduction of the funding-bond scheme. Indeed, even after negotiations for rescheduling were broken off in May 1934, the creditors were considering a German offer to issue funding bonds at reduced interest rates or to repurchase coupons for cash at 40 percent of face value. It is thus hard to believe that bondholders were expecting an all-or-nothing payout, and the equality between marginal and average values is thus at variance with the Bulow-Rogoff model.

Setting aside this evidence against the model, assume for the moment that it is valid. What would it imply about the size of the German gains from the buybacks? The Bulow-Rogoff criterion says that Germany gained from the buybacks, as the right-hand side now equals 1, but it also says that the gains cannot have been large. Bulow and Rogoff (1988) use as a suitable upper bound for the variable q the partial debt-service payments that creditors have been able to extract. On the basis of data in Harris (1935, p. 114) and Hoffmann, Grumbach, and Hesse (1965, p. 828), I find that Germany transferred 1.6 percent of its national income to its creditors in 1932 and 1.1 percent in 1933. Furthermore, the average secondary-market price of German debt in New York was 32 percent in 1932 and 41 percent in 1933. Therefore, the cost of the buybacks given by the left-hand side of the Bulow-Rogoff criterion is between 0.5 percent and 1 percent smaller than the benefit—not a very large margin of gain.

The 1930s and the 1980s: Bank Debt Versus Bond Debt

The finding that marginal and average values were equal for Germany is completely different from the corresponding findings for the 1980s. The cross-country regressions of Cohen (1989) and, especially, of Claessens et al. (1990) show that most debtor countries were on the

---

[54] The models of Claessens and Diwan (1989) and Cohen (1991a, pp. 70-71) imply that marginal and average values are equal only when there is no risk of default. This is because they assume a linear enforcement technology whereby the creditor can extract a constant proportion of output in the event of default. On this assumption, the lender always gets something when default occurs, which means that marginal and average values cannot be equal if default can occur. The more general framework of Bulow and Rogoff (1991) allows for the possibility that the creditor cannot extract resources in the event of default.

horizontal portion of the Debt Laffer Curve in the 1980s, where the marginal value of the debt is zero. The authors of these studies conclude that open-market buybacks cannot reduce the market value of the debt and are therefore undesirable. One possible explanation for the difference in findings may lie in the fact that my results apply to the secondary market for bonds, whereas Cohen and Claessens et al. are concerned with sovereign debt, which is largely owed to banks.

It is also noteworthy that relatively little of the defaulted short-term bank debt was repurchased in the German case. This can be adduced from the figures for repurchases of scrip and blocked marks in Table 6, which show that they were smaller than repurchases of bonds. Because repurchases of defaulted short-term debt occurred in the blocked-mark market and some of the repurchases recorded in Table 6 were purchases of blocked marks created to pay interest on long-term bond debt, repurchases of defaulted short-term debt must have been smaller than the numbers in the amount of blocked-mark repurchases recorded in Table 6. There is no obvious reason for bond-debt values to respond to buybacks differently than bank-debt values. The difference in the German case may perhaps reflect the fact that banks can easily coordinate a decision to write off debt and bondholders cannot.

Summary

To recapitulate, the model of buybacks developed by Bulow and Rogoff (1988) says that a debtor country cannot gain from a buyback, because the marginal value of its debt is usually below the average price actually paid on the secondary market. Its loss from the buyback is signaled by an increase in the market price of the remaining debt. When German buybacks were at their height, secondary-market prices increased strongly, so strongly in fact that the market value of the debt remained unchanged despite the large buybacks, and some calculations suggest that it increased. The market value of Bolivian debt behaved similarly during the 1988 buyback. My statistical analysis, however, rejects the hypothesis that the German buybacks themselves reduced the market value of German debt by less than they reduced the face value. It rejects even more decisively the stronger hypothesis that a debtor like Germany can be on the "wrong side" of the Debt Laffer Curve, where the marginal value of the debt is negative and buybacks cause its market value to rise. In fact, the marginal and average values of the debt were shown to be equal, a result that guaranteed some small benefit to Germany even in the context of the Bulow-Rogoff model.

In the German case, however, the fact that the two values are equal is actually evidence against the model itself. First, the equality occurs jointly with a positive relation between buyback expenditures and secondary-market prices, a joint result that cannot occur in the Bulow-Rogoff model. Second, Germany's creditors cannot have been expecting an all-or-nothing payout, which is what the equality means in the Bulow-Rogoff model.

My findings confirm the conclusion Eichengreen and Portes (1989b, p. 82) reached with regard to the Chilean case in the 1930s, that "the time series behavior of bond prices suggests that, while repurchases put upward pressure on prices, the effects were not particularly large." In fact, my analysis adduced no evidence at all of any upward pressure, and my results are based on the behavior of prices for 96 bonds, whereas they dealt with only 1.

The evidence so far has not suggested that Germany gained significantly from the buybacks. It has merely established that marginal and average values did not differ in the way required to show that Germany lost. Yet evidence exists that the buybacks were seen at the time to be beneficial to both sides. Although the creditors objected to the buybacks, they were aware that they were benefiting from them. Thus, we read that "German manufacturers and German debtors are benefited, as also are the foreign creditors, the holders of German dollar bonds, the demand for which at improved prices has been considerably increased as a result of these transactions."[55] It remains to be seen, therefore, whether there were additional ways in which Germany and its creditors may have gained—or, more exactly, have expected to gain—from the buybacks. My attempt to estimate the German Debt Laffer Curve points in that direction. It suggests that Germany and its creditors attached different valuations to German debt. I turn now to the reasons.

---

[55] BAK R2/253 (Handakten Könning), Copy of "Opening Statement of the Creditor Representatives, Berlin," May 4, 1934; FRBNY, German Government File, "Crane to Kenzel," April 6, 1933.

4 WHY DID THE BUYBACKS TAKE PLACE?

The formal analysis in the previous section suggests that the German economy did not lose from the buybacks, which did not merely transfer foreign exchange to the creditors. Yet the gains from the buybacks measured in that context seem to be very small. Certainly, they are not large enough to support the traditional view, found in Ellis (1941) and Childs (1958), that German practices in the foreign-exchange market, including the buybacks, represented a successful form of monopolistic exploitation. Are there reasons to believe that the formal framework neglects or underestimates some of the gains from the buybacks?

One partial explanation for the buybacks is that German companies are thought to have made large accounting profits from them.[56] In this respect, the situation resembles the Chilean case in the 1980s, in which Larraín (1989) found that companies could make large profits from buybacks. This explanation, however, cannot account for the behavior of the German government, which could impose its will on business whenever it felt that business was gaining at the government's expense. It actually did so in January 1934, when it promulgated regulations that tightly controlled the amount of foreign exchange available for buybacks.

The historical literature offers an alternative explanation by treating the buybacks as export subsidies (Doering, 1969, pp. 196-199). The economic literature also offers justifications in suggesting that the debtor's subjective valuation of the probability of repudiation may have been higher than the creditors' valuation (Claessens and Diwan, 1989, p. 263), and that the costs of repudiation may have been higher for the debtor than for the creditor, causing the debtor to value a unit of debt more highly. A variant of the second argument is that, when the costs of repudiation fall over time, so that the debtor's inducement to repudiate rises steadily, buying back debt may nevertheless be cheaper for the debtor than facing the trade-disruption penalty that will be imposed if the debtor repudiates. A buyback may be mutually beneficial under these conditions by postponing repudiation and by allowing it to occur only when it is less costly to the debtor (Kenen, 1991).

---

[56] NA RG59 862.51/3849, "Dispatch No. 490 from the American Embassy, Berlin," January 31, 1934.

Additional Exports or Debt Reduction?

As we have seen, earlier accounts of the buyback operations assumed that they were intended to subsidize exports. The subsidy consisted of issuing rationed foreign exchange to exporters so that they could purchase German bonds in New York, sell them in Berlin, and profit from the difference between the New York and Berlin prices. I have cited evidence showing that reduction of the foreign debt was an equally important motive. More evidence to this effect can be obtained by using cointegration methods to test whether the buybacks were, in reality, a covert export subsidy. I summarize my work and discuss it in greater detail in Appendix C.

That using cointegration methods is an appropriate procedure follows from the evidence shown in Figure 1. Although no discernible tendency is shown for arbitrage to equalize New York and Berlin prices, the two prices track each other closely enough for one to suspect that they are cointegrated. As both the New York and Berlin series exhibit unit roots (Table 10), the appropriate method of looking for a long-run relation between them is to test for cointegration. The results in Table 10 suggest that the series are indeed cointegrated.[57] The long-run static equation in Table 10 provides us with the result of primary interest. Because the average Berlin price from 1932 to 1934 was almost exactly 80, the equation predicts an average New York price just slightly above 40.

Conceivably, the equation merely reflects the overvaluation of the mark, but that hypothesis is hard to test. Calculation of the degree of overvaluation would be a daunting task, because German price indices reflect the effects of almost complete price control. There is evidence that, when a devaluation was contemplated, the number discussed was 30 percent, which was the degree of overvaluation assumed by the German Finance Ministry. If we accept that figure as the actual degree of overvaluation, the gap between bond prices in New York and Berlin

---

[57] The residuals from a regression of the New York price on the Berlin price were tested for stationarity using the augmented Dickey-Fuller test, following Engle and Granger (1987). The appropriate critical value is 3.17, rejecting narrowly the null hypothesis of no cointegration. The reader should note, however, that, when there is no time trend in the initial regression, cointegration is not present. As the power of these tests is low in small samples (Campbell and Perron, 1991), the procedures followed should be regarded as a way to measure the relation between the two prices rather than as definite proof that they are separately nonstationary and are cointegrated. The tests for cointegration from Johansen (1988) used in the next section strongly accept the hypothesis that there is a cointegrating vector, but the estimated vector has the nonsensical implication that the Berlin price is below the New York price.

TABLE 10

Relation between the New York and Berlin Prices of 6 Percent Bonds

Unit-Root Tests

Variable	Test	Result	Critical Value
nyw	DF test	−2.04	−3.60
nyw	ADF test	3.21	4.86
$berlinw$	DF test	−1.42	−3.60
$berlinw$	ADF test	2.93	4.86

The critical values for the standard Dickey Fuller (DF) test are for the case in which a constant and trend appear in the regression. Those for the augmented Dickey-Fuller (ADF) test are for the case of a constant and no trend.

Cointegration Test

$$u_t = -0.407u_{t-1} + 0.550\Delta u_{t-1} - 0.141\Delta u_{t-2} .$$
$$\quad\ (3.553) \qquad (5.034) \qquad\ (2.011)$$

The ADF statistic is 3.558; its critical value is 3.2 (Engle and Yoo, 1987, table 3) ; t-statistics are in parentheses.

Long-Run Static Equation

$$nyw_t = 21.826 + 0.230\,berlinw_t .$$
$$\qquad\ (9.862) \ \ (0.115)$$

The Wald Test Chi-squared statistic is 1089.2; standard errors are in parentheses.

OLS Regression in Error-Correction Form

$$nyw_t = 0.443\Delta nyw_{t-1} + 0.247\Delta berlinw_t - 0.073\,ecm_{t-1} .$$
$$\qquad\ (3.445) \qquad\quad (2.655) \qquad\quad (3.763)$$

$R^2 = 0.432$, $F(3,37) = 9.4$, $DW = 1.79$; t-statistics are in parentheses.

AR 1-3: $F(3,34) = 1.19$; ARCH 3: $F(3.31) = 0.40$; RESET: $F(1,36) = 2.66$; the Normality Chi-squared statistic is 0.39.

AR 1-3 is the Harvey (1981) test for up to third-order autocorrelation; ARCH 3 is the Engle (1982) test for squared autocorrelated residuals; RESET is the Ramsey (1969) test of the specification against linear combinations of the regressors; the Normality Chi-squared statistic tests whether the observations are normally distributed using the Jarque-Bera (1980) statistic.

implies that the additional export procedure could more than compensate an exporter for the overvaluation of the mark. Citing the pervasive shortage of foreign exchange, however, the Economics Ministry believed that additional exports financed by bond buybacks were profitable only when the New York price was 40 percent of the Berlin price.[58] Thus, the long-run equation shows that the buybacks could not have been desirable, given the official German view regarding export subsidies. By implication, the additional export procedures were either an inappropriate way to subsidize exports or were justified by another purpose, namely, redeeming the debt.

More telling evidence for the contention that trade policy did not determine debt policy can be found in the fact that debt buybacks were lowest during the period in which German exports were expanded most successfully. Under the New Plan, running from September 1934 to November 1936, exports increased by 19 percent (Petzina, 1977, p. 123). There is thus no clear link between bond purchase and export promotion.

Divergent Valuations between Debtor and Creditor

The present value of a liability is obtained by discounting the sum of expected repayments. Differences in valuation between debtors and creditors can therefore arise when assessments regarding the probability of repayment differ or when the amounts paid by a debtor differ from those received by the creditors (Claessens and Diwan, 1989, p. 262). Scrutiny of confidential documents helps us to decide whether the first possibility can explain the German buybacks, because it can uncover systematic differences in valuation between the Germans and their creditors of which the creditors may have been ignorant. The second possibility may also be important, because Germany, being in partial default, was in danger of suffering trade penalties. If the costs of these penalties to Germany were likely to exceed the gains, they would drive a wedge between the two parties' valuations of the debt. This issue can be addressed by examining the type and pattern of sanctions threatened by the creditors.

Differing Perceptions Concerning Default

Contemporary sources state that "the mere fact that the Germans are eager to buy back securities sold to foreigners is convincing evidence that they believe current quotations in foreign markets underestimate

---

[58] BAK R2/14216, "State Secretary Posse to von Krosigk," March 28, 1934.

42

the value of various German issues." This undervaluation was attributed to "uncertainty concerning Germany's ability and willingness to transfer interest payments in the future" and to the universal belief that Germany was about to move from default to repudiation.[59]

In actual fact, Hitler had decided explicitly from the outset, with no dissent from his cabinet, not to repudiate the entire debt irrevocably but to manipulate the situation to Germany's benefit.[60] An anonymous source within the German government informed the American creditors of this decision but without revealing the crucial fact of the Führer's endorsement.[61] The creditors found it hard to penetrate the workings of the Nazi regime to determine who was actually in charge of international financial policy (Forbes, 1987, p. 323; Schröder, 1970, p. 181). They perceived a threat to their interests from the "party extremists," but the threat could not materialize as long as Hitler opposed repudiation.

The decision to continue some form of debt service, even if only by payments into blocked accounts from which the prospect of acquiring dollars was limited, was never reversed. Even in mid-1939, when severe difficulties in servicing dollar debt were anticipated, the Economics Ministry advised converting the interest and principal then falling due into a new class of *schlechtes wertpapiere*, rather than repudiating the obligations. At precisely this time, however, foreign creditors were expecting repudiation.[62]

Another reason for the difference in assessing the likelihood of default was the creditors' skepticism about the viability of the Nazi economic program. It has often been remarked that Hitler's prediction of a return to full employment was very accurate and that foreign commentators were surprised when their own predictions of immediate collapse were confounded (James, 1986, p. 344). These differences in assessment led to "sharp" disagreements between German and creditor spokesmen over the value of the "defaulted" bonds.[63] It is thus evident

[59] *Journal of Commerce*, December 8, 1932; AA SW, Finanzielle Beziehungen mit der USA, "Report on German Credit in New York," November 30, 1932.

[60] DGFP, Series C, Vol. 1, No. 182, "Meeting of the Economic Policy Committee," April 24, 1933, in which Hitler is recorded as having stated that there was no interest in a full cancellation of German debts; Schröder (1970, p. 79); Weinberg (1970, p. 46).

[61] FRBNY, Committee on German Foreign Credits File, "Letter to Herbert Case," June 14, 1933.

[62] BAK R7/3411, "Report on German Foreign Economic Relations [in 1938]," in section on "Transferpolitik" (pp. 83-84), n.d.; "Foreign Bond Default Trend Seen Growing," *The New York Times*, July 6, 1939.

[63] An example is the exchange between the mayor of Hamburg, Krogmann, and the British statesman Lord Lloyd, recorded in Krogmann's diaries (Krogmann, 1977, p. 93).

that the creditors were unaware of German intentions with regard to default and more pessimistic about the German economy than the situation warranted. They did appear to realize at times that German threats of default were meant merely to drive down bond prices in order to facilitate buybacks. Ramsey MacDonald personally taxed the German ambassador with this accusation while in a "bitter mood against Germany."[64] MacDonald's suspicions were confirmed by Hitler himself, who gloated in his table talk over the success of the plan, attributed to Schacht, to drive down bond prices and use middlemen for the buybacks (Picker, 1977, p. 332). The success of the plan, however, depended crucially on maintaining secrecy about the buybacks. Otherwise, the operation itself would have revealed information to the creditors and driven up bond prices (Claessens and Diwan, 1989).

Did the Germans actually succeed in systematically concealing their operations? They made every attempt to do so. Ambassador Hans Luther blithely denied that buybacks were taking place even as Swiss and Dutch banks operated on Wall Street as buyers for their German clients. New York knew that $38 million of repurchases were carried out in the first four months of 1933, of which all but $3.5 million were conducted by Swiss and Dutch intermediaries.[65] These repurchases, however, represented only a small proportion of the buybacks recorded in Table 6 that Schacht reported to the German cabinet. Later, during the 1934 negotiations, the creditors admitted that they had "no way of verifying the table [on buybacks] presented to us."[66] Later records of successful secret buybacks exist. In 1939, facing the irate owners of Austrian bonds, the Foreign Ministry observed that the "Americans do not know and should not know" that buybacks had been taking place.[67]

Lloyd claimed the bonds were worthless; Krogmann stated that German trade would revive and foreign-exchange payments would be resumed. Krogmann was a typical representative of the German industrial and shipping interests involved in bond repurchases.

[64] BAK R43II/787, "Telegram from the German Ambassador in London," June 23, 1934.

[65] NA RG59 862.51/3635, "Questionnaire No. 6," May 26, 1933; FRBNY, Standstill File, Division of West European Affairs, "Moffat to Phillips," June 22, 1933.

[66] Dulles Papers, Box 13, Berlin Conference File, "Statement of the Creditors' Committee," from the "Report of Pierre Jay, Laird Bell, and W.W. Cumberland on the German Debt Conference of April-May 1934," Annex 8, May 2, 1934.

[67] AA Ha Pol, Finanzielle Beziehungen mit der USA, "Discussion on the Handling of Austrian Dollar Loans," February 23, 1939.

The qualitative evidence thus indicates that the buybacks were carried out secretly, with the aid of third parties, and that their true extent was unknown to the creditors. To test this conclusion more rigorously, I ask whether the creditors would have been able to forecast future bond prices, given the information available to them.

According to Dulles, creditors were able to acquire from a "confidential source" information on the planned monthly movements of German foreign-exchange reserves during 1933.[68] The creditors used these figures to indicate the extent of the buybacks. The data shown in Figures 2 and 3, taken together, suggest that bond prices did indeed increase when German reserves were falling. Although Dulles seems to have had none of this information available in 1934, the report of one of the Creditors' Subcommittees states that they had access to the supposedly secret German planned foreign-exchange balance for the first half of 1934.[69]

These reserve movements can be deemed to reflect planned buybacks because the Reichsbank routinely allocated part of the planned monthly foreign-exchange outflow for future buybacks under the *zusatzausfuhr* system.[70] But some of the foreign-exchange receipts were used for other purposes, such as the purchase of strategic war materials. Hence, the reserve movements should be correlated with the buybacks but should not match them exactly. Furthermore, actual reserve movements have unplanned components, reflecting exogenous shocks, even though the authorities were trying as far as possible to control the monthly foreign-exchange balance.

These qualifications notwithstanding, creditors could have used their knowledge of planned foreign-exchange outflows to forecast buybacks and thus to buy German bonds in anticipation of the higher prices the buybacks would produce. A test of this hypothesis, focused on the forecastability of secondary-market prices, is thus a test of whether the creditors had accurate inside information about future buybacks.

---

[68] Dulles Papers, Box 12, "Memorandum by Mr. Loree," May 20, 1933, contains nine months of these figures and an attempt to work out what they implied about the extent of the buybacks.

[69] Dulles Papers, Box 13, Berlin Conference File, Copy of "Report of the Creditors' Subcommittee on Statistics," May 2, 1934. The planned balance appears in BAK R2/227 (Handakten Könning), "Finanzierung der Ausfuhrförderung," August 16, 1934.

[70] BAK R2/229 (Handakten Könning), "Foreign-Exchange Balance for Germany," September 3, 1934, contains details of foreign exchange allocated for planned buybacks by means of additional exports; BAK R7/4706, "Circular No. 21852/32," July 27, 1932, states that it would take about a month to get approval for and carry out a specific *zusatzausfuhr* operation.

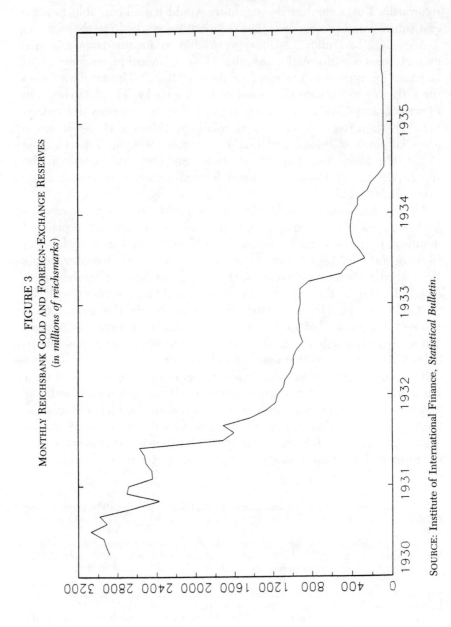

FIGURE 3

MONTHLY REICHSBANK GOLD AND FOREIGN-EXCHANGE RESERVES
(*in millions of reichsmarks*)

SOURCE: Institute of International Finance, *Statistical Bulletin.*

I have therefore tested the hypothesis that the expected change in the bond price between two dates depends upon the known movement in German reserves during the interval between those dates. I assume that the reserve movement was known before the beginning of the interval, because the information was leaked or purloined from the Reichsbank. Using p and r to represent the logarithms of the changes in bond prices and reserves,

$$E(p_t) - E(p_{t-1}) = c + \alpha(r_t - r_{t-1}) + u_t . \tag{4}$$

Following, for example, Mishkin (1990), rational expectations are imposed by assuming that

$$E(p_t) = p_t + e_t , \tag{5}$$

where e_t is the forecast error of the secondary-market price and is assumed to be orthogonal to any information known at time t. Substituting back into equation (4),

$$\Delta p_t = c + \Delta r_t + u_t , \tag{6}$$

where $u_t = e_t - e_{t-1}$. This model exhibits first-order autocorrelation, and the lagged error can be correlated with past values of r because rational expectations do not rule out the correlation of e_t with information known at time t, such as information about r_t. Therefore, the model is estimated by a maximum-likelihood technique. The tests described in Appendix C indicate that the secondary-market prices and reserves are nonstationary and are not cointegrated, which calls for a specification in differences, as recorded in Table 11. The dummy variable cb in the maximum-likelihood equation allows for the influence of the large credit repayments made by the Reichsbank in March 1933 (James, 1985, p. 253), but it turns out to be insignificant and is omitted from the next equation. The forecasting properties of the next equation are good, as is indicated by the low values of the t-statistics for the forecasts (that is, standardized forecast errors).

How much of an advantage did this inside information really confer? To answer this question, I estimated an unconstrained vector auto-regression covering the entire period for which data are available (June 1930 to October 1935),[71] and I compared the performance of this

---

[71] Data on Reichsbank reserves were published quarterly in the *Statistical Bulletin* published by the Institute of International Finance, New York University, for the Investment Bankers Association of America. The data are used here because they would have been readily available to creditors.

TABLE 11
PROPERTIES OF THE FORECASTING EQUATION FOR GERMAN BOND PRICES

Unit-Root Tests

ADF test statistics: 3.2 for log nya, 0.001 for log res.
The critical value is 4.65.

Tests for Cointegration

ADF test statistic using Engle-Granger method: 2.80.

Maximum Eigenvalue and Trace Statistics:

	Max Eigenvalue	Trace
Test statistic	11.16	13.49
Critical value	14.04	15.20

OLS Regression

$$\Delta\log nya_t = -0.001 + 0.756\Delta\log res_t \ .$$
$$\quad\quad\quad\quad (0.07) \quad (2.27)$$

$R^2 = 0.126$; $DW = 1.29$; t-statistics are in parentheses.
Test for second-order autocorrelation: $F(2,38) = 26.92$.

Maximum-Likelihood Estimation

$$\Delta\log nya_t = 0.021 + 0.178\Delta\log res_t + 0.502e_{t-1} - 0.270e_{t-2} + e_t \ .$$
$$\quad\quad\quad (1.03) \quad (2.18) \quad\quad\quad\quad (2.94) \quad\quad\quad (1.79)$$

$$\Delta\log nya_t = 0.013 + 0.162\Delta\log res_t + 0.078cb_t + 0.542e_{t-1} - 0.303e_{t-2} + e_t \ .$$
$$\quad\quad\quad (0.77) \quad (2.07) \quad\quad\quad\quad (0.66) \quad (3.42) \quad\quad\quad (1.96)$$

t-statistics are in parentheses.

One-Step-Ahead Forecasts

Date	Forecast Standard Error	t-Statistic
1935: 7	0.0935	–0.0763
1935: 8	0.0935	–0.7741
1935: 9	0.0941	0.1462
1935:10	0.0937	0.3124

equation with the performance of the maximum-likelihood equation shown in Table 11, which incorporates advance knowledge of reserve movements. The exercise asks whether the forecasting performance of the vector autoregressive regression (VAR) estimated over the longest period possible dominates that of the "secrecy" model estimated over the buyback period alone. Table 12 shows the relevant results. Despite the larger number of observations, the forecast performance of the VAR, as measured by the forecast errors, is far inferior to that of the "secrecy" equation, which allows for advance knowledge of reserves.

It thus appears that financial espionage was sufficient to provide information that creditors could have used to forecast the effects of buybacks on bond price. By implication, the creditors had useful inside

TABLE 12

FORECASTING BOND PRICES FROM AN UNCONSTRAINED VAR USING THE FULL SAMPLE, 1930:6 TO 1935:10

Tests for Cointegration

Maximum Eigenvalue and Trace Statistics:

	Max Eigenvalue	Trace
Test statistic	5.01	5.18
Critical value	14.04	15.20

Vector Autoregression Equations

Dependent Variable	$\Delta\log res_{t-1}$	$\Delta\log res_{t-2}$	$\Delta\log nya_{t-1}$	$\Delta\log nya_{t-2}$
$\Delta\log res_t$	0.190	0.077	0.106	0.134
	(0.130)	(0.062)	(0.175)	(0.084)
$\Delta\log nya_t$	0.021	0.061	0.196	0.079
	(0.096)	(0.096)	(0.129)	(0.129)
$F(2,56)$	1.00	0.31	1.13	0.39

The vector alienation coefficient is 0.86663; the trace correlation is 0.26041. Standard errors are in parentheses.

One-Step-Ahead Forecasts

Date	Forecast Standard Error	t-Statistic
1935:7	0.109	0.131
1935:8	0.115	0.615
1935:9	0.113	1.144
1935:10	0.113	0.892

49

information about the buybacks themselves, and the successful conceal-
ment of the actual buybacks was not sufficient to prevent creditors
from driving up prices. It seems, then, that the secrecy argument does
not explain how Germany benefited from the buybacks and cannot
explain the strong negative correlation found in my cross-sectional
equations regressing changes in market value on face values repurchased.

Different Costs of Default

Even when debtors and creditors agree on the likelihood of default, they
may value debt differently, because penalties for repudiation may punish
the debtor without bringing comparable benefits to the creditor. In this
section, I assume that the creditors know with certainty that the debtor
will repudiate in full at a certain date in the future. The secondary-
market discount will then be determined by the sum of the present
values of the resources the creditor can acquire in the event of default
and the stream of payments until the default occurs, expressed as a
fraction of the present value of the face value of the debt. If the
penalty for repudiation is a forfeiture of assets and both parties know
it, their valuations of the debt will be identical (Kenen, 1991). This
follows intuitively from the fact that the seizure of a tangible asset
reduces the debtor's wealth by the same amount as it raises the creditor's wealth. If trade disruption is the penalty, however, the debtor will
lose unambiguously but the creditor will not gain.[72] Trade disruption
has asymmetrical effects, and the debtor, who suffers more than the
creditor, will thus value the debt more highly and will therefore gain
from a secondary-market buyback (Claessens and Diwan, 1989, p. 263).
Hence, theory predicts that a debtor is more likely to buy back debt
from a creditor who threatens trade retaliation than from a creditor
who threatens asset seizure.

This prediction is verified in the German case. There is much
evidence to suggest that the Germans were extremely worried about
the threat of asset seizure. Before the transfer moratorium of July
1933, they tried to remove what assets they could from the creditor
countries. The concern reappears in late 1939 with regard to the
possible seizure of German assets by New York banks.[73] Even more

---

[72] The creditors may also lose by sacrificing trade income, but there is no reason to
assume that the trade losses will be the same for the debtor and the creditors.

[73] DGFP, Series C, Vol. 1, No. 211, "Circular of the Foreign Ministry Circulated
Secretly by Karl Ritter, Head of the Foreign Ministry Economic Department, to All
German Legations," May 5, 1933; AA Ha Pol, Anleihen und Wertpapiere, Finanzwesen
2, "Ausländische Nachrichtenagenturen," December 20, 1939.

credible was the threat by the Netherlands, Switzerland, and Britain to attach trade revenues, as all three countries had current-account surpluses with Germany.[74] Before entering the 1933 negotiations, the Swiss delegates privately noted their strength in this regard and later noted the potential for coordinating strategy with the Netherlands and Britain.[75] Schacht knew that the state of Swiss-German and Dutch-German trade made this a credible threat and that he had no choice but to sign the special transfer agreements favoring the Swiss and Dutch creditors.[76] The French also had a trade surplus with Germany and successfully used the same threat to prevent discrimination against their citizens holding the Dawes and Young loans.[77] The British obtained similar treatment when they broke their joint front with the Americans after the Berlin Conference of May 1934. Like the seizure of assets, however, the seizure of trade revenues is fully symmetrical in its effects. Trade disruption is not, but it was the most credible threat available to the Americans.

Seizure of trade revenues by the United States was not an important threat because U.S. imports from Germany were small. Dulles, the American negotiator, noted that "the position of the U.S. bondholder is extremely weak." He was aware that the United States could institute an "economic warfare system" against Germany but that this would not benefit U.S. bondholders. Hence, prohibiting important exports to Germany such as sales of copper wire to a German electrical utility, was the measure actually considered.[78] Such an embargo could not have benefited the United States, but it would have harmed Germany, as cheaper wire was not available elsewhere. The U.S. chargé d'affaires in Berlin went further in describing the drastic effects of U.S. trade retaliation, which, "in the case of a country which has to import so

[74] Attachment of trade revenues would have been carried out by setting up a clearing house for all payments to German exporters. The clearing house would then confiscate a certain proportion of the payments. Clearly, the creditor countries could suffer certain losses from the resulting interference with trade. The argument is thus dependent on these losses being very small or on their being offset by expanded trade with third parties.

[75] *Documents Diplomatiques Suisses*, Vol. 10 (1982), No. 229, "Procès-Verbal de la Séance du 15 Juin 1933"; Vol. 11 (1983), No. 373, "Le Ministre de Suisse à la Haye à la Division du Commerce," March 12, 1934.

[76] BAK R43II/32940, "Schacht to State Secretary Lammers," November 27, 1933.

[77] *Documents Diplomatiques Français*, Vol. 6 (1966), No. 242, "Ministre des Affaires Étrangères Barthou aux Ambassadeurs de France à Berlin et Londres," May 26, 1934.

[78] Dulles Papers, Box 12, "Report of John Foster Dulles on the Berlin Debt Discussions of December 1933," December 23, 1933; FRBNY, Committee on German Foreign Credits File, "Meeting of July 14, 1934."

much of its raw material as does this, would obviously mean so great a lowering of wages as to wreck the German standard of living and foster discontent very dangerous to the Government."[79] In fact, the general tenor of Secretary of State Hull's policy made an embargo unlikely. Hull sought to reach a trade agreement with Germany, indeed to practice "economic appeasement" as a way to alleviate political tensions, which he believed to be at root economic (Schröder, 1970, pp. 140, 168). Nevertheless, the German Foreign Office was worried by the prospect of American trade retaliation.[80]

Given these differences in the stances of the creditor countries, theory tells us not to expect German buybacks in the Netherlands and Switzerland, which threatened to seize German earnings from foreign trade, but rather to expect them in the United States, which threatened trade disruption. That is, in fact, what happened. Although a country-by-country breakdown of buybacks has not been found, it is evident that the larger part took place in the United States. At the end of 1936, Germany possessed 35 percent of the German bonds issued in the United States (a figure that did not include cancellations by German companies), and these represented about 62 percent of all German bond buybacks. Yet the issues in the United States accounted for only 49 percent of total German long-term debt. Furthermore, a country-by-country breakdown of buybacks does exist for dollar-denominated bonds. Most of these were issued in the United States, but 16 percent were issued in other countries, according to German Foreign Office files. And, although 35 percent of all U.S. issues were in German hands by the end of 1936, only 19 percent of the Dutch dollar-denominated issue and none of the Swiss or British dollar issues had been repurchased.[81] One should also note that there is no record of buybacks in Switzerland before 1938 or of buybacks of guilder-denominated bonds. It is thus evident that the threat of trade disruption, with its asymmetrical effects, influenced German policy. Buybacks were concentrated in the one country that threatened trade disruption in the event of repudiation.

---

[79] NA 862.51/3954, "White to the Secretary of State," April 5, 1934.

[80] BAK R2/4058, "Berger to Prause," March 24, 1936.

[81] AA Ha Pol, Anleihen und Wertpapiere, Anmeldstelle für Auslandsschulden, "Auf laufende deutsche Auslandsschulden," June 3, 1936.

5 CONCLUSION

Despite the large body of work on the interwar debt crisis, (summarized in Eichengreen, 1991), the case of Germany, the largest defaulter, has not been studied by economists. The present study has attempted to fill this gap and to exploit the information found about the causes and effects of sovereign debt repurchases.

Implications for the Bulow-Rogoff Buyback Model

The German experience of the 1930s constitutes a crucial historical experiment for those interested in studying open-market buybacks. In no other instance was the volume of buybacks so large or such a large proportion of global debt outstanding. Furthermore, the buybacks were conducted entirely at the debtor's initiative, with none of the negotiated elements associated with recent episodes or, indeed, with other buybacks in the 1930s. At no time did the creditors agree that Germany should set aside revenues to buy back debt, and no outside agency provided the necessary funds. Even in this pure case, however, the argument advanced by Bulow and Rogoff (1988, 1990, 1991), that buybacks will not benefit the debtor, is not supported by the empirical evidence. This has been demonstrated despite the fact that the market value of German debt remained unchanged during the intense buyback activity from 1932 to 1934, a finding that is consistent, *a priori*, with the predictions of the Bulow-Rogoff model. This conclusion is consistent with the further finding that the marginal and average values of German debt were equal in this period, a finding that conflicts with the Bulow-Rogoff framework. An equality of values can occur in that framework only when creditors expect an all-or-nothing payout, which was not true of Germany's creditors.

The rejection of the Bulow-Rogoff model is reinforced by our knowledge of other circumstances pointing to the possibility that Germany gained from the buybacks. In particular, the geographical distribution of the buybacks shows that they may have been a response to U.S. threats of trade retaliation. Models that distinguish between trade retaliation and asset seizure, such as the one proposed by Kenen (1991), illuminate an important facet of the buyback decision.

Implications for the Economic History of the Third Reich

The buybacks did not reflect a bout of National-Socialist irrationality. Even if one does not accept my argument that the evidence tells against the Bulow-Rogoff model, the equality between the marginal and average values of the debt implies that the buybacks conferred a welfare gain on Germany. Thus, the somewhat skeptical assessment of German debt policy by James (1986, p. 412) has not been confirmed by my findings. My study nevertheless rejects the traditional argument that the buybacks benefited the Nazi economy by subsidizing exports in the context of a complex bilateral trading system. Furthermore, the gains made by the management of the foreign debt emerge in a framework completely different from that used in the early studies by Hirschman (1945) and Childs (1958), who employed concepts of bilateral monopoly.

Did the buybacks contribute to the economic recovery of Germany after the Second World War? This is a complex question. One must ask how the February 1953 London Agreement, which finally achieved a settlement with Germany's creditors, might have looked in the absence of the buybacks. Hermann Abs, Adenauer's debt negotiator, said that "the Schachtian policy of buying back unserviced loans below par contributed to crushing Germany's moral standing with the creditors" (Schwarz, 1982, p. 60). There is some evidence, however, that the creditors also benefited from the buybacks, a finding that would invalidate Abs' assertion. Indeed, it should be noted that the creditors did not demand compensation for having sold their bonds at depressed prices (Foreign Bondholders Protective Council, 1952). The London Agreement itself reduced the prewar debt to 38 percent of its face value in 1931, and this is close to the discount on the debt prevailing when the buybacks took place: an average of 35 percent in 1932 and 41 percent from 1932 to 1934 (Boelcke, 1985, p. 205). It is thus possible to conclude that Germany might have done better to conserve its scarce foreign-exchange earnings and to leave the entire debt to be settled after the war. The clauses of the London Agreement were complex, however, and precise analysis should be a topic for further research.

Implications for Research on the International Debt Problem

Buybacks were almost unknown in the 1800s, common in the 1930s, and practiced only on a small scale in the 1980s.[82] The present study

---

[82] Aggarwal (1989) refers to a plan by Mexico to repurchase its debts by a secret buyback in the 1820s.

can offer some support to the advocates of open-market buybacks. The fact that the market value of the debt remained unchanged after the German buybacks cannot be linked to the buybacks themselves. Yet the special conditions of the 1930s, the potential for trade disruption in a world divided politically and economically, helped to make the buybacks attractive. Another characteristic of the time, however, the secrecy imposed by a totalitarian dictatorship, did not decisively influence the outcome of the buybacks. It would appear that creditors acquired knowledge that they could use to forecast secondary-market prices. This result contradicts the suggestion by Eichengreen (1991) that secrecy was important for the success of buybacks in the 1930s.

Recent research by Garber (1990) and English (1991) suggests that reputational considerations played an important role in the resolution of U.S. debt crises during the eighteenth and nineteenth centuries. The present study has found that buybacks can be an important part of such a process. The most important implication for the current debt situation lies in the fact that the German buybacks of the 1930s involved largely bonds rather than bank loans. This suggests that countries like Mexico that have issued exit bonds could benefit from repurchasing them at a discount. Recent estimates of the Debt Laffer Curve suggest that there would be no gain from open-market buybacks, but the estimates are derived from data pertaining to bank loans. Buybacks of the German type can come into play as a solution to the debt problem once the debts of developing countries have been converted into bonds.

It must nevertheless be pointed out that some of the results reported here rely on a unique but limited set of cross-sectional data. The archives may yet yield better time series on German repurchases than the crude annual series I have developed and presented in this study. Finding such data and relating it to the evolution of secondary-market prices will be necessary to resolve the issues completely.

APPENDIX A
SOURCES ON THE SIZE OF THE BUYBACKS

Table 6 is built on the assumption that all details on the size of buy-backs appearing in officially published sources are almost certainly false (for example, the statistics reported in Harris, 1935, appendix 12).

Confidential German data relating to buybacks appear in four guises: (1) unpublished balance-of-payments statistics, (2) statistics on revenue from additional export procedures involving buybacks, (3) statistics on expenditure on additional export procedures, (4) other more informal statements on the buybacks contained in memoranda, minutes, and so on. The year-by-year construction of Table 6 was carried out as follows:

For 1938 to 1941. From the balance-of-payments accounts for those years in R7/3629, which gives capital outflows from debt and blocked-mark repurchases; R7/3068 provides further explanation.

For 1936 to 1937. From the profits on additional export procedures recorded by the Anmeldstelle für Auslandsschulden (R2/31032-31034, 14217); the statement of the finance minister to Schacht that these receipts averaged RM 75 million per year provides additional evidence. As Ellis (1941, p. 198) points out, these figures were calculated from the formula 100(*loss from export*)/*discount*. This formula is used to find the appropriate discount when the losses are taken from Ellis (1941, p. 235); the discount is multiplied by the figures for expenditure on additional exports to produce the buyback figure. No breakdown between blocked-mark and bond repurchases is available; it is therefore assumed that the proportions are the same as they were in 1935.

For 1935. The figure for the small amount of bond buybacks is from R2/14208 ("Posse to von Krosigk," undated). The figure for scrip and blocked-mark repurchases is taken from the monthly expenditures recorded in R2/30132 (minus the amount recorded as being for bond repurchases); it is multiplied by the discount in Ellis (1941, p. 397).

For 1934. From R2/229 (Handakten Könning) "Foreign Exchange Balance for Germany," September 3, 1934, which gives the exchange balance for the first six months of the year. As there are no figures for the remainder of the year, this may be an understatement. Although information about planned repurchases exists, whether or not the repurchases took place cannot be verified.

For 1933. From R2/14208, which contains a figure for buybacks made by means of additional exports; a Foreign Ministry document (Creditors' Subcommittee on Statistics, in Dulles Papers, Box 13, Berlin Conference File) gives a figure for those buybacks that did not use the additional-export mechanism.

For 1932. No independent figure exists for this year. The estimate in Table 6 is the residual obtained from the estimate of total buybacks through 1936 made by the U.S. Department of Commerce, and from the estimates described above for the period from 1933 to 1936; see the discussion in the text.

APPENDIX B
THE SIMPLEST MODEL OF BUYBACKS

A very simple model will prove the contentions in the text. Assume that the debtor country's output Q is a random variable the cumulative distribution of which is given by GQ with support 0, ∞. The penalty for default is a fractional loss, a, of output, and the level of output at which it is worthwhile to default is Q°. The face value of the debt is D, and the face value of the amount bought back is X. The market value of the debt to risk-neutral creditors then depends on what accrues to them in the default and nondefault states:

$$V = \int_0^{Q^{\circ}} aQ\,dG(Q) + \int_{Q^{\circ}}^{\infty} (D - X)\,dG(Q) \ ,$$

and $Q^{\circ} = (1/a)(D - X)$. The marginal value of the debt is

$$p_m = \frac{\partial V}{\partial D} = \int_{Q^{\circ}}^{\infty} dG(Q) = 1 - G^* \ .$$

The average price at which lenders are prepared to sell the debt is

$$p = \frac{V}{D - X} = \int_0^{Q^{\circ}} \frac{aQ}{D - X}\,dG(Q) + 1 - G \ .$$

Clearly, the marginal value is below the average price, because lenders take the default penalty into account when choosing the price at which they will be prepared to sell a unit of debt.

It remains to prove that the average price of the debt and, hence, the value of the remaining debt must rise when debt is bought back. Differentiating with respect to p, X,

$$\frac{\partial p}{\partial X} = \frac{a}{(D - X)^2} \int_0^{Q^{\circ}} Q\,dG(Q) + \left(1 - \frac{1}{D - X}\right) Q^* \ .$$

Multiplying through by $D - X$ gives the result.

APPENDIX C
DETAILS OF THE TIME-SERIES TESTS

This Appendix provides a brief discussion of the tests for cointegration applied to the series for New York and Berlin bond prices and those for Reichsbank reserves and German bond prices in New York. The references in the text contain complete expositions of these matters.

The tests for the two bond prices, shown in Table 10, follow the methodology in Engle and Granger (1987). The first test used is a unit-root test for the residuals of a regression of the Berlin price on the New York price. The second step is the estimation of the stationary relation between the two prices, the existence of which is isomorphic to the presence of cointegration. It is derived from the solution to an ordinary-least-squares regression of the New York price on the Berlin price and on its lagged value. It satisfies a Wald test found by Bardsen (1988) to be valid for testing the significance of the equation, and the standard errors indicate that the coefficients are significant as well. This is the relation of interest to us. As the Berlin price was 80 on average from 1932 to 1934, the equation implies a long-run New York price of 41.5.

The short-run dynamic of the relation between the two bond prices is shown by the equation at the bottom of Table 10. All the variables are significant, and the regression includes an error-correction term ($ecm_t = nyw_t - \alpha berlin\ w_t$) describing the adjustment of the U.S. bond price to the German bond price. This equation passes a number of diagnostic tests, including those for autocorrelation of up to the third order, for autoregressive conditional heteroscedasticity (ARCH), and for omitted variables (RESET). The significance of the error-correction term shows that the cointegrating relations are valid. The negative sign on the error-correction term, however, suggests that the relation between the two prices evinces significant mean reversion. Thus, any deviation from the long-run relation that increased the *bondsspanne* would only temporarily make additional exports more desirable.

A different approach is used to test for cointegration between Reichsbank reserves and the New York bond prices. It is based on Johansen (1988). Let H_t be an $(n \times 1)$ vector of $I(1)$ variables, the dynamic behavior of which is captured by the following autoregressive model:

$$H_t = \Pi_t H_{t-1} + \Pi_2 H_{t-2} + ... \Pi_p H_{t-p} + \varepsilon_t \ ,$$

where the errors are

$$\Pi N_n(0,\ \Sigma)\ .$$

This system can be rewritten in first-difference form:

$$\Delta H_t = \Pi H_{t-1} + \Gamma_1 \Delta H_{t-1} + ... + \Gamma_{p-1}\Delta H_{t-p+1} + \varepsilon_t \ ,$$

where

$$\Gamma_i = -(\Pi_{i+1} + \Pi_{i+2} + \Pi_p)\ ,\ i = 1\ ,...,\ p - 1\ ,$$

and where

$$\Pi = \Pi_1 + \Pi_2\ ... + \Pi_p - I\ .$$

If the variables in H are cointegrated, then rank $(\Pi) = q < p$, and there exist $(p \times q)$ matrices α and β such that $\Pi = \alpha\beta'$. The number of cointegrating vectors β is q. The αs represent the vectors of adjustment parameters in the error-correction mechanism, but they were not measured in the text because Π was found to have rank $q = p = 2$ (that is, no cointegration was present). Johansen (1988) developed a maximum-likelihood procedure to estimate the α and β coefficients and derived two statistics to test for the number of cointegrating vectors. These are called "trace" and "maximum eigenvalue" in Tables 11 and 12. This procedure performs better than the Engle-Granger (1987) method in small samples (Gonzalo, 1989) and is therefore preferred here.

In Table 11, the test is performed for the VAR with an unrestricted constant. The critical values are taken from Johansen (1989, table T1, p. 83). As a Lagrange-multiplier test records strong evidence of second-order autocorrelation, the model is estimated with a second-order autoregressive error process. The model shows that reserves are a small but significant determinant of the bond price. In fact, only first-order autocorrelation is significant in this estimation, despite the results of the Lagrange-multiplier test, thus confirming the original specification.[83]

As the Johansen tests for the null hypothesis of no cointegrating vectors are accepted, the VAR is therefore differenced, and the results

---

[83] The skeptical reader is invited to ignore the rational-expectations interpretation of this regression and to treat it as an attempt to estimate a standard autoregressive integrated moving average (ARIMA) forecasting model in which the change in reserves is a one-period leading indicator.

are shown in Table 12. Standard tests on the parameters show them to be insignificant for the most part. The values of the vector alienation coefficient (analogous to $1 - R^2$) and trace correlation (analogous to R^2) likewise show that the fit is poor.

REFERENCES

Archives

Bank of England:
  German Country Files (OV34)
Bundesarchiv Koblenz (BAK):
  Reich Finance Ministry Files (R2)
  Reich Economics Ministry Files (R7)
  Reich Chancellery Files (R43II)
Federal Reserve Bank of New York (FRBNY):
  Committee on German Foreign Credits File
  German Country File
  German Government File
  Standstill File
National Archives of the United States (NA)
  General Records of the Department of State, Record Group 59, Decimal
    File 862.51 (RG59)
  Bureau of Foreign and Domestic Commerce, General Records, Commercial
    Attaché's Reports, Record Group 151 (RG151)
Politisches Archiv des Auswärtigen Amtes (AA):
  Sonderreferat Wirtschaft (SW), –1936
  Handelspolitisches Abteilung (Ha Pol), 1937–
Seeley G. Mudd Library, John Foster Dulles Papers, Princeton University,
  Princeton, New Jersey

Other

Aggarwal, Vinod, "Interpreting the History of Mexico's Debt Crises," in Barry
  Eichengreen and Peter Lindert, eds., *The International Debt Crisis in
  Historical Perspective*, Cambridge, Mass., MIT Press, 1989, pp. 140-188.
Bardsen, Gerrit, "The Estimation of Long-Run Coefficients from Error-
  Correction Models," *Oxford Bulletin of Economics and Statistics*, 51 (No. 4,
  1988), pp. 345-350.
Barkai, Avraham, *From Boycott to Annihilation: The Economic Struggle of
  German Jews: 1933-43*, Hanover and London, University Press of New
  England, 1989.
Berkenkopf, Paul, "Probleme der deutschen Grosseisenindustrie," *Wirtschafts-
  dienst*, 17, (June 3, 1932), pp. 739-742.
Boelcke, Willi A., *Die Kosten von Hitlers Krieg: Kriegsfinanzierung und
  finanzielles Kriegserbe in Deutschland 1933-1948*, Paderborn, Schöningh,
  1985.

Bonnell, Alan Thomas, *German Control over International Economic Relations*, Urbana, University of Illinois Press, 1940.

Bouchet, Michel H., and Jonathan Hay, "The Rise of the Market-Based Menu Approach and Its Limitations," in Ishrat Husain and Ishac Diwan, eds., *Dealing with the Debt Crisis*, Washington, D.C., World Bank, 1989, pp. 146-162.

Bulow, Jeremy, and Kenneth Rogoff, "The Buyback Boondoggle," *Brookings Papers on Economic Activity* (No. 2, 1988), pp. 675-698.

———, "Cleaning up Third World Debt without Getting Taken to the Cleaners," *The Journal of Economic Perspectives*, 4 (No. 1, 1990), pp. 31-42.

———, "Sovereign Debt Repurchases: No Cure for Overhang," *Quarterly Journal of Economics*, 106 (No. 4, 1991), pp. 1219-1235.

Campbell, John Y., and Pierre Perron, "Pitfalls and Opportunities, What Macroeconomists Should Know About Unit Roots," *NBER Macroeconomics Annual*, 3 (1991), pp. 52-79.

Childs, Frank C., *The Theory and Practice of Exchange Control in Germany*, The Hague, Martinus Nijhoff, 1958.

Claessens, Stijn, "The Debt Laffer Curve: Some Estimates," Washington, D.C., World Bank, 1988, processed.

Claessens, Stijn, and Ishac Diwan, "Market-Based Debt Reduction," in Ishrat Husain and Ishac Diwan, eds., *Dealing with the Debt Crisis*, Washington, D.C., World Bank, 1989, pp. 258-272.

Claessens, Stijn, Ishac Diwan, Kenneth Froot, and Paul Krugman, *Market Based Debt Reduction for Developing Countries: Principles and Prospects*, Policy and Research Series No. 16, Washington, D.C., World Bank, 1990.

Cohen, Daniel, "How to Cope with a Debt Overhang: Cut Flows Rather than Stocks," in Ishrat Husain and Ishac Diwan, eds., *Dealing with the Debt Crisis*, Washington, D.C., World Bank, 1989, pp. 229-235.

———, *Private Lending to Sovereign States: A Theoretical Autopsy*, Cambridge, Mass., MIT Press, 1991a.

———, "Secret Buybacks of LDC Debt," CEPR Discussion Paper No. 424, London, Centre for Economic Policy Research, 1991b.

Dengg, Soren, Deutschlands Austritt aus dem Völkerbund und Schachts "Neuer Plan," Frankfurt and New York, Lang, 1986.

Documents Diplomatiques Françaises, Vol. 6, Paris, Imprimerie Nationale, 1966.

Documents Diplomatiques Suisses, Vols. 10, 11, Bern, Benteli, 1982, 1983.

Documents on German Foreign Policy (DGFP), Series C, Vol. 1, Washington, D.C., Government Printing Office, 1957.

Doering, Doerte, "Deutsche Aussenwirtschaftspolitik 1933-1935: Die Gleichschaltung der Aussenwirtschaft in der Frühphase des nationalsozialistischen Regimes," doctoral diss., Free University of Berlin, 1969.

Eichengreen, Barry, "Historical Research on International Lending and Debt," *The Journal of Economic Perspectives*, 5 (No. 2, 1991), pp. 149-169.

Eichengreen, Barry, and Peter Lindert, eds., *The International Debt Crisis in*

Historical Perspective, Cambridge, Mass., MIT Press, 1989.

Eichengreen, Barry, and Richard Portes, "After the Deluge: Default, Negotiation and Adjustment in the Interwar Years," in Barry Eichengreen and Peter Lindert, eds., *The International Debt Crisis in Historical Perspective*, Cambridge, Mass., MIT Press, 1989a, pp. 12-37.

——, "Dealing with Debt: The 1930s and the 1980s," in Ishrat Husain and Ishac Diwan, eds., *Dealing with the Debt Crisis*, World Bank, Washington, D.C., 1989b, pp. 69-86.

——, "Settling Defaults in the Era of Bond Finance," *The World Bank Economic Review*, 3 (No. 2, 1989c), pp. 211-239.

Einzig, Paul, *Germany's Default: The Economics of Hitlerism*, London, Macmillan, 1934.

Ellis, Howard S., *Exchange Control in Central Europe*, Cambridge, Mass., Harvard University Press, 1941.

Engle, Robert, "Autoregressive Conditional Heteroscedasticity with Estimates of the Variance of United Kingdom Inflation," *Econometrica*, 50 (No. 3, 1982), pp. 987-1007.

Engle, Robert, and Clive W. Granger, "Co-integration and Error Correction: Representation, Estimation and Testing," *Econometrica*, 55 (No. 2, 1987), pp. 251-276.

Engle, Robert, and Byung Sam Yoo, "Forecasting and Testing in Cointegrated Systems," *Journal of Econometrics*, 35, (No. 1, 1987), pp. 143-159.

English, William B., "When America Defaulted, American State Debts in the 1840s," University of Pennsylvania, 1991, processed.

The Fitch Bond Book, New York, Fitch, 1935.

Forbes, Neil, "London Banks, the German Standstill Arrangements and Economic Appeasement in the 1930s," *The Economic History Review*, 40 (No. 4, 1987), pp. 571-587.

Foreign Bondholders Protective Council, *Annual Report*, New York, Foreign Bondholders Protective Council, 1936, 1952.

Garber, Peter, "Alexander Hamilton's Market Based Debt Reduction Plan," Carnegie-Rochester Conference Series on Public Policy, 35 (Autumn 1991), pp. 79-100.

Gonzalo, Jesus, "Comparison of Five Alternative Methods of Estimating Long-Run Equilibrium Relationships," Discussion Paper 89-55, Department of Economics, University of California, San Diego, 1989.

Harris, Charles Reginald Schiller, *Germany's Foreign Indebtedness*, London, Humphrey Milford, 1935.

Harrod, Roy F., *The Life of John Maynard Keynes*, London, Macmillan, 1951.

Harvey, Andrew C., *The Econometric Analysis of Time Series*, Oxford, Philip Allan, 1981.

Heckman, James J., "Sample Selection Bias as a Specification Error," *Econometrica*, 47 (No. 1, 1979), pp. 153-161.

Hirschman, Albert O., *National Power and the Structure of Foreign Trade*, Berkeley, University of California Press, 1945.

Hoffman, Walter G., Franz Grumbach, and Helmut Hesse, *Das Wachstum der deutschen Wirtschaft seit der Mitte des 19. Jahrhunderts*, Berlin and Heidelberg, Springer, 1965.

Homer, Sydney, and Richard Sylla, *A History of Interest Rates*, New Brunswick, N.J., Rutgers University Press, 1989.

Institut für Konjunkturforschung, *Konjunkturstatistisches Jahrbuch*, Berlin, Institut für Konjunkturforschung, 1930-1936.

James, Harold, *The Reichsbank and Public Finance in Germany 1924-1933: A Study of the Politics of Economics during the Great Depression*, Frankfurt, Fritz Knapp, 1985.

———, *The German Slump*, Oxford, Oxford University Press, 1986.

Jarque, Carlos M., and Anil K. Bera, "Efficient Tests for Normality, Homoscedasticity and Serial Independence of Regression Residuals," *Economic Letters*, 6 (No. 3, 1980), pp. 255-259.

Johansen, Soren, "Statistical Analysis of Cointegrating Vectors," *Journal of Economic Dynamics and Control*, 12 (No. 2-3, 1988), pp. 231-254.

———, *Likelihood Based Inference on Cointegration: Theory and Applications*, Bologna, Centro Universitario di Econometria, 1989.

Jorgensen, Erika, and Jeffrey Sachs, "Default and Renegotiation of Latin American Foreign Bonds in the Interwar Period," in Barry Eichengreen and Peter Lindert, eds., *The International Debt Crisis in Historical Perspective*, Cambridge, Mass., MIT Press, 1989, pp. 48-85.

Kenen, Peter B., "Debt Buybacks and Forgiveness in a Model with Voluntary Repudiation," *International Economic Journal*, 5 (No. 1, 1991), pp. 1-13.

Klug, Adam, "The Theory and Practice of Reparations and American Loans to Germany," Working Papers in International Economics G-90-03, International Finance Section, Department of Economics, Princeton University, Princeton, N.J., 1990.

———, "The German Buybacks, 1932-39: A Cure for Overhang?" Working Papers in International Economics G-90-03, International Finance Section, Department of Economics, Princeton University, Princeton, N.J., 1992.

Krogmann, Carl Vincent, *Es ging um Deutschlands Zukunft, Erlebtes täglich diktiert von dem früheren Regierenden Bürgermeister von Hamburg*, Leoni am Starnberger See, Druffel, 1977.

Krugman, Paul, "Market Based Debt Reduction Schemes," in Jacob A. Frenkel, Michael P. Dooley, and Peter Wickham, eds., *Analytical Issues in Debt*, Washington, D.C., International Monetary Fund, 1989, pp. 258-278.

Kuczynski, Robert R., *Deutsche Anleihen im Ausland*, Berlin, Brookings Institution, 1928.

Larraín, Felipe, "Debt Reduction Schemes and the Management of Chilean Debt," Internal Discussion Paper, Washington, D.C., World Bank, 1989.

McNeil, William C., *American Money and the Weimar Republic: Economics and Politics on the Eve of the Great Depression*, New York, Columbia University Press, 1986.

Maddala, G.S., *Limited-Dependent and Qualitative Variables in Econometrics*,

Cambridge and New York, Cambridge University Press, 1983.

Mishkin, Frederick, "Is the Fisher Effect for Real? A Reexamination of the Relationship between Inflation and Real Interest Rates," National Bureau of Economic Research Working Paper No. 3632, Cambridge, Mass., National Bureau of Economic Research, 1990.

Neal, Larry, "The Economics and Finance of Bilateral Clearing Agreements: Germany, 1934-38," *The Economic History Review*, 32, (No. 3, 1979), pp. 391-404.

Petzina, Dietmar, *Die deutsche Wirtschaft in der Zwischenkriegszeit*, Stuttgart, Steiner, 1977.

Picker, Henry, ed., *Hitlers Tischgespräche im Führerhauptquartier*, 2nd ed., Stuttgart, Seewald, 1977.

Ramsey, J.B., "Tests for Specification Errors in Classical Linear Least-Squares Regression Analysis, "*Journal of the Royal Statistical Society*, 31 (Series B), pp. 350-357.

Ritschl, Albrecht, "Die deutsche Zahlungsbilanz 1936-41 und das Problem des Devisenmangels vor Kriegsbeginn," *Vierteljahreshefte für Zeitgeschichte*, 39 (No. 2, 1991), pp. 103-123.

Royal Institute of International Affairs, *The Problem of International Investment*, London, Oxford University Press, 1937.

Schröder, Hans Jürgen, *Deutschland und die Vereinigten Staaten 1933-1939: Wirtschaft und Politik in der Entwicklung des deutsch-amerikanischen Gegensatzes*, Wiesbaden, F. Steiner, 1970.

Schuker, Stephen A., *American "Reparations" to Germany, 1919-1933: Implications for the Third-World Debt Crisis*, Princeton Studies in International Finance No. 61, International Finance Section, Department of Economics, Princeton University, Princeton, N.J., 1988.

Schwarz, Hans-Peter, ed., *Die Wiederherstellung des deutschen Kredits: Das Londoner Schuldenabkommen*, Stuttgart, Belser, 1982.

Temin, Peter, "Soviet and Nazi Planning in the 1930s," *Economic History Review*, 44 (No. 4, 1991), pp. 573-593.

Vella, Frank, "A Simple Estimator for Simultaneous Models with Censored Endogenous Regressions," Appendix B, Working Paper No. 199, Department of Economics, University of Rochester, Rochester, 1989.

——, "A Simple Estimator for Simultaneous Models with Censored Endogenous Regressions," *International Economic Review*, 34 (No. 2, 1993), pp. 441-457.

Weinberg, Gerhard L., The Foreign Policy of Hitler's Germany: Diplomatic Revolution in Europe, 1933-36, Chicago, University of Chicago Press, 1970.

White, Halbert, "A Heteroscedasticity-Consistent Covariance Matrix and a Direct Test for Heteroscedasticity," *Econometrica*, 48 (No. 4, 1980), pp. 817-838.

Zimmerman, Carl, "Währungsverfall und Umverschuldung," *Wirtschaftsdienst*, 23 (November 10, 1933), pp. 1548-1550.

PUBLICATIONS OF THE
INTERNATIONAL FINANCE SECTION

Notice to Contributors

The International Finance Section publishes papers in four series: ESSAYS IN INTER-NATIONAL FINANCE, PRINCETON STUDIES IN INTERNATIONAL FINANCE, and SPECIAL PAPERS IN INTERNATIONAL ECONOMICS contain new work not published elsewhere. REPRINTS IN INTERNATIONAL FINANCE reproduce journal articles previously published by Princeton faculty members associated with the Section. The Section welcomes the submission of manuscripts for publication under the following guidelines:

ESSAYS are meant to disseminate new views about international financial matters and should be accessible to well-informed nonspecialists as well as to professional economists. Technical terms, tables, and charts should be used sparingly; mathematics should be avoided.

STUDIES are devoted to new research on international finance, with preference given to empirical work. They should be comparable in originality and technical proficiency to papers published in leading economic journals. They should be of medium length, longer than a journal article but shorter than a book.

SPECIAL PAPERS are surveys of research on particular topics and should be suitable for use in undergraduate courses. They may be concerned with international trade as well as international finance. They should also be of medium length.

Manuscripts should be submitted in triplicate, typed single sided and double spaced throughout on 8½ by 11 white bond paper. Publication can be expedited if manuscripts are computer keyboarded in WordPerfect 5.1 or a compatible program. Additional instructions and a style guide are available from the Section.

How to Obtain Publications

The Section's publications are distributed free of charge to college, university, and public libraries and to nongovernmental, nonprofit research institutions. Eligible institutions may ask to be placed on the Section's permanent mailing list.

Individuals and institutions not qualifying for free distribution may receive all publications for the calendar year for a subscription fee of $35.00. Late subscribers will receive all back issues for the year during which they subscribe. Subscribers should notify the Section promptly of any change in address, giving the old address as well as the new.

Publications may be ordered individually, with payment made in advance. ESSAYS and REPRINTS cost $8.00 each; STUDIES and SPECIAL PAPERS cost $11.00. An additional $1.25 should be sent for postage and handling within the United States, Canada, and Mexico; $1.50 should be added for surface delivery outside the region.

All payments must be made in U.S. dollars. Subscription fees and charges for single issues will be waived for organizations and individuals in countries where foreign-exchange regulations prohibit dollar payments.

Please address all correspondence, submissions, and orders to:

International Finance Section
Department of Economics, Fisher Hall
Princeton University
Princeton, New Jersey 08544-1021

67

List of Recent Publications

A complete list of publications may be obtained from the International Finance Section.

ESSAYS IN INTERNATIONAL FINANCE

157. Wilfred J. Ethier and Richard C. Marston, eds., with Charles P. Kindleberger, Jack Guttentag, Richard Herring, Henry C. Wallich, Dale W. Henderson, and Randall Hinshaw, *International Financial Markets and Capital Movements: A Symposium in Honor of Arthur I. Bloomfield.* (September 1985)

158. Charles E. Dumas, *The Effects of Government Deficits: A Comparative Analysis of Crowding Out.* (October 1985)

159. Jeffrey A. Frankel, *Six Possible Meanings of "Overvaluation": The 1981-85 Dollar.* (December 1985)

160. Stanley W. Black, *Learning from Adversity: Policy Responses to Two Oil Shocks.* (December 1985)

161. Alexis Rieffel, *The Role of the Paris Club in Managing Debt Problems.* (December 1985)

162. Stephen E. Haynes, Michael M. Hutchison, and Raymond F. Mikesell, *Japanese Financial Policies and the U.S. Trade Deficit.* (April 1986)

163. Arminio Fraga, *German Reparations and Brazilian Debt: A Comparative Study.* (July 1986)

164. Jack M. Guttentag and Richard J. Herring, *Disaster Myopia in International Banking.* (September 1986)

165. Rudiger Dornbusch, *Inflation, Exchange Rates, and Stabilization.* (October 1986)

166. John Spraos, *IMF Conditionality: Ineffectual, Inefficient, Mistargeted.* (December 1986)

167. Rainer Stefano Masera, *An Increasing Role for the ECU: A Character in Search of a Script.* (June 1987)

168. Paul Mosley, *Conditionality as Bargaining Process: Structural-Adjustment Lending, 1980-86.* (October 1987)

169. Paul A. Volcker, Ralph C. Bryant, Leonhard Gleske, Gottfried Haberler, Alexandre Lamfalussy, Shijuro Ogata, Jesús Silva-Herzog, Ross M. Starr, James Tobin, and Robert Triffin, *International Monetary Cooperation: Essays in Honor of Henry C. Wallich.* (December 1987)

170. Shafiqul Islam, *The Dollar and the Policy-Performance-Confidence Mix.* (July 1988)

171. James M. Boughton, *The Monetary Approach to Exchange Rates: What Now Remains?* (October 1988)

172. Jack M. Guttentag and Richard M. Herring, *Accounting for Losses On Sovereign Debt: Implications for New Lending.* (May 1989)

173. Benjamin J. Cohen, *Developing-Country Debt: A Middle Way.* (May 1989)

174. Jeffrey D. Sachs, *New Approaches to the Latin American Debt Crisis.* (July 1989)

175. C. David Finch, *The IMF: The Record and the Prospect.* (September 1989)

176. Graham Bird, *Loan-loss Provisions and Third-World Debt.* (November 1989)

177. Ronald Findlay, *The "Triangular Trade" and the Atlantic Economy of the Eighteenth Century: A Simple General-Equilibrium Model.* (March 1990)
178. Alberto Giovannini, *The Transition to European Monetary Union.* (November 1990)
179. Michael L. Mussa, *Exchange Rates in Theory and in Reality.* (December 1990)
180. Warren L. Coats, Jr., Reinhard W. Furstenberg, and Peter Isard, *The SDR System and the Issue of Resource Transfers.* (December 1990)
181. George S. Tavlas, *On the International Use of Currencies: The Case of the Deutsche Mark.* (March 1991)
182. Tommaso Padoa-Schioppa, ed., with Michael Emerson, Kumiharu Shigehara, and Richard Portes, *Europe After 1992: Three Essays.* (May 1991)
183. Michael Bruno, *High Inflation and the Nominal Anchors of an Open Economy.* (June 1991)
184. Jacques J. Polak, *The Changing Nature of IMF Conditionality.* (September 1991)
185. Ethan B. Kapstein, *Supervising International Banks: Origins and Implications of the Basle Accord.* (December 1991)
186. Alessandro Giustiniani, Francesco Papadia, and Daniela Porciani, *Growth and Catch-Up in Central and Eastern Europe: Macroeconomic Effects on Western Countries.* (April 1992)
187. Michele Fratianni, Jürgen von Hagen, and Christopher Waller, *The Maastricht Way to EMU.* (June 1992)
188. Pierre-Richard Agénor, *Parallel Currency Markets in Developing Countries: Theory, Evidence, and Policy Implications.* (November 1992)
189. Beatriz Armendariz de Aghion and John Williamson, *The G-7's Joint-and-Several Blunder.* (April 1993)
190. Paul Krugman, *What Do We Need to Know About the International Monetary System?.* (July 1993)

PRINCETON STUDIES IN INTERNATIONAL FINANCE

56. Paul De Grauwe, Marc Janssens, and Hilde Leliaert, *Real-Exchange-Rate Variability from 1920 to 1926 and 1973 to 1982.* (September 1985)
57. Stephen S. Golub, *The Current-Account Balance and the Dollar: 1977-78 and 1983-84.* (October 1986)
58. John T. Cuddington, *Capital Flight: Estimates, Issues, and Explanations.* (December 1986)
59. Vincent P. Crawford, *International Lending, Long-Term Credit Relationships, and Dynamic Contract Theory.* (March 1987)
60. Thorvaldur Gylfason, *Credit Policy and Economic Activity in Developing Countries with IMF Stabilization Programs.* (August 1987)
61. Stephen A. Schuker, *American "Reparations" to Germany, 1919-33: Implications for the Third-World Debt Crisis.* (July 1988)
62. Steven B. Kamin, *Devaluation, External Balance, and Macroeconomic Performance: A Look at the Numbers.* (August 1988)
63. Jacob A. Frenkel and Assaf Razin, *Spending, Taxes, and Deficits: International-Intertemporal Approach.* (December 1988)

64. Jeffrey A. Frankel, *Obstacles to International Macroeconomic Policy Coordination*. (December 1988)
65. Peter Hooper and Catherine L. Mann, *The Emergence and Persistence of the U.S. External Imbalance, 1980-87*. (October 1989)
66. Helmut Reisen, *Public Debt, External Competitiveness, and Fiscal Discipline in Developing Countries*. (November 1989)
67. Victor Argy, Warwick McKibbin, and Eric Siegloff, *Exchange-Rate Regimes for a Small Economy in a Multi-Country World*. (December 1989)
68. Mark Gersovitz and Christina H. Paxson, *The Economies of Africa and the Prices of Their Exports*. (October 1990)
69. Felipe Larraín and Andrés Velasco, *Can Swaps Solve the Debt Crisis? Lessons from the Chilean Experience*. (November 1990)
70. Kaushik Basu, *The International Debt Problem, Credit Rationing and Loan Pushing: Theory and Experience*. (October 1991)
71. Daniel Gros and Alfred Steinherr, *Economic Reform in the Soviet Union: Pas de Deux between Disintegration and Macroeconomic Destabilization*. (November 1991)
72. George M. von Furstenberg and Joseph P. Daniels, *Economic Summit Declarations, 1975-1989: Examining the Written Record of International Cooperation*. (February 1992)
73. Ishac Diwan and Dani Rodrik, *External Debt, Adjustment, and Burden Sharing: A Unified Framework*. (November 1992)
74. Barry Eichengreen, *Should the Maastricht Treaty Be Saved?*. (December 1992)
75. Adam Klug, *The German Buybacks, 1932-1939: A Cure for Overhang?*. (November 1993)

SPECIAL PAPERS IN INTERNATIONAL ECONOMICS

15. Gene M. Grossman and J. David Richardson, *Strategic Trade Policy: A Survey of Issues and Early Analysis*. (April 1985)
16. Elhanan Helpman, *Monopolistic Competition in Trade Theory*. (June 1990)
17. Richard Pomfret, *International Trade Policy with Imperfect Competition*. (August 1992)
18. Hali J. Edison, *The Effectiveness of Central-Bank Intervention: A Survey of the Literature After 1982*. (July 1993)

REPRINTS IN INTERNATIONAL FINANCE

25. Jorge Braga de Macedo, *Trade and Financial Interdependence under Flexible Exchange Rates: The Pacific Area*; reprinted from *Pacific Growth and Financial Interdependence*, 1986. (June 1986)
26. Peter B. Kenen, *The Use of IMF Credit*; reprinted from *Pulling Together: The International Monetary Fund in a Multipolar World*, 1989. (December 1989)
27. Peter B. Kenen, Transitional Arrangements for Trade and Payments Among the CMEA Countries; reprinted from *International Monetary Fund Staff Papers* 38 (2), 1991. (July 1991)